THE B OUNCEBACK
Artist

THE 8-STEP SECRET TO CONQUERING
LIFE'S SETBACKS

Susan Baroncini-Moe, M.A.

YES PRESS

Indianapolis, Indiana

"Once every few years a book comes along with an insight so penetrating, so powerful, and so demonstrably true that it instantly changes the way we think. Such a book is The BounceBack Artist. It isn't the number of times life knocks you down, it's the number of times you get back up, and Susan's experience and wisdom will benefit everyone who reads her book."

- Robert Thomas Bethel, author of *Strengthen Your Business: Fail-Proof Strategies from the Man Who Has Rescued 77 Businesses*

"Setbacks are inevitable but bouncebacks must be intentional. This book takes the mystery out of how to rebound more quickly and positively. It will give you helpful ideas successful, healthy people use that you can use to deal with life's challenges."

- Mark Sanborn, author of *The Fred Factor* and *The Potential Principle*

"Susan sets a new standard for rebounding from life's setbacks with a smart mix of wisdom, mindfulness, positivity, and practicality. If you've had a setback, whether at work on in your personal life, The BounceBack Artist is your path to getting back on track."

- Ellen Petry Leanse, bestselling author of *The Happiness Hack*

"As a business owner and entrepreneur, this book is one of the most effective and pragmatic I have seen to help leaders get unstuck. The Bounceback Artist is a tremendous tutorial in how to lift yourself up from a setback or something you may perceive as a defeat. Susan's transparency and compassion are entirely evident and compelling. I recommend this book to anyone who is looking to get better (personally and professionally) and enlighten the way they see this rollercoaster we call life!"

- Shelli A. Herman, President and Founder, Shelli Herman and Associates, Inc.

"There are lots of books about having a positive attitude, and that's all well and good. But in The Bounceback Artist, Susan Baroncini-Moe gives us an actual step-by-step plan that can help anyone overcome adversity and create opportunity from challenges. This book goes beyond feel-good platitudes. It provides an actual strategy for action that can turn your life in a productive, positive direction. Buy this book. It's a game-changer!"

- Joe Calloway, author of *The Leadership Mindset*

"Susan really gets it! A setback can happen to anyone, especially those in the entrepreneurial space. This book has a clear, effective process to finding your way back from a setback. A must read for anyone who wants to get back to business, fresh and without baggage."

- Steven Hoffman, author of *Make Elephants Fly: The Process of Radical Innovation, Captain and CEO of Founders Space*

"Learning how to overcome personal and professional setbacks and put them behind you quickly is a trait of successful, happy people. The Bounceback Artist makes this overwhelming process manageable by breaking it down into tangible steps called the REBOUNDS program. The advice and homework in each step of the plan will help you deal with the complex emotions of setbacks, learn about yourself and get your life back on track in no time. It will even help you be better prepared for future challenges.

Susan Baroncini-Moe is no stranger to setbacks herself, and her personal perspective is proof you can overcome adversity and come out stronger on the other side. Drawing on her own story as well as those of her many clients over the years, her advice is direct, compassionate and actionable. There isn't a person among us who would not benefit from reading The Bounceback Artist."

- Brande Plotnick, healthcare brand and product marketer

"Everybody has career setbacks or plateaus, but high achievers know how to process negative feedback to change and grow in order to reach the next level. This book is like having Susan Baroncini-Moe as your personal coach, guiding you from a place of denial and negativity to a place of joy and empowerment. Highly recommended!"

- Kevin Kruse, New York Times bestselling author and CEO,

LEADx

"Life will knock you back on your ass at times. That's when we all need a coach in our corner barking at us to 'Get back up! Get back up!'. I am happy to say your coach is right here, in this book you hold in your hands. Get ready to punch life's challenges right in the nose."

- Mike Michalowicz, author of *Clockwork* and *Profit First*

"Anyone who's had or will have a setback (i.e. everyone) should read this book. Business expert Susan Baroncini-Moe's profoundly practical plan provides a sorely needed roadmap for overcoming life's inevitable difficulties."

- Zach Mercurio, Bestselling Author of *The Invisible Leader: Transform Your Life, Work, and Organization with the Power of Authentic Purpose*

"Obstacles are not the problem...how we deal with them is. Susan provides a unique and effective 8 step process to help anyone through anything."

- Matt Manero, author of *You Need More Money!*

"Inspirational, insightful, and empowering, The Bounce-Back Artist provides a practical, step-by-step plan for getting rid of the brain junk that gets in the way of success. As a trusted friend and gifted coach, Susan Baroncini-Moe brings clarity into getting back in the game when life throws us off course."

- Ben Cope, CEO of Internet Genius Consulting

"*The BounceBack Artist* is a rare opportunity to delve into an acclaimed life coach's revealing personal journey and learn tools —in an easy-to-digest step-by-step program—that will move you forward. It's the next best thing to one-on-one coaching with the amazing Susan—honest, sage advice that motivates as it enlightens and focuses you on processing your past and planning for your future, one that is full of possibility and promise."

- Julie Cantor, MD, JD, Founder & CEO of Harlan and Adjunct Faculty, UCLA School of Law

Susan is a master at helping you identify what's holding you back, why it's holding you back, and how to overcome it. She has the ability to just "get" you, even if she's never met you, and in *The BounceBack Artist*, she meets you where you are with actionable steps you can take to not only bounce back, but become the best possible you. If you're ready to bounce back, you smply can't go wrong with Susan's guidance."

- Stephanie Hinderer, Publisher of *Curl* Magazine

Ellen Bass: "Change," by Ellen Bass , copyright © by Ellen Bass. Reprinted by permission of the author.

Library of Congress Cataloging-in-Publication Data: LCCN: 2018914090
ISBN 13 PB: 978-0-578-41539-0
ISBN 13 Ebook: 978-0-9822793-9-7

Table of Contents

To my clients over the years who have put
their faith in me to guide them along their path:

"Promise me you'll always remember:
You're braver than you believe,
and stronger than you seem,
and smarter than you think."

- Christopher Robin to Winnie the Pooh

Change
by Ellen Bass

This is where I yank the old roots
from my chest, like tomatoes
we let grow until December, stalks
thick as saplings.

This is the moment when the ancient fears
race like thoroughbreds, asking for more
and more rein. And, I, the driver,
for some reason they know nothing of
strain to hold them back.

Terror grips me like a virus
and I sweat, fevered,
trying to burn it out.

This feat is so invisible. All you can see
is a woman going about her ordinary day,
drinking tea, taking herself to the movies,
reading in bed. If victorious
I will look exactly the same.

Yet I am hoisting a car from mud ruts
half a century deep. I am hacking
a clearing through the fallen slash
of my heart. Without laser precision,
with only the primitive knife of need, I cut
and splice the circuitry of my brain.
I change.

PREFACE

MOST PEOPLE WHO KNOW me or have read about me probably think I lead a charmed, easy life: I own a successful business, I'm married to a real, live rock star, and we live in a nice home with our two super adorable dogs (seriously, check my Instagram feed, @suebmoe — they're ridiculously cute). I've broken a Guinness World Record and appeared on national TV, hosted four podcasts and written a bestselling book.

I imagine that most people think these things came easy to me. My dad was a doctor, so I grew up with many advantages: I had plenty of nice things and went to private school. I also have the privilege that comes with being white, so all in all it probably seems like life has been pretty smooth sailing. And in some respects, it has.

Except the story I've shared in these short paragraphs doesn't give you the whole picture. I have Attention Deficit Hyperactivity Disorder (ADHD), which went undiagnosed until I was in my mid-30s, and I often refer to my early 20s as "The Dark Years" because of just how depressed and troubled I was during those few years. Perhaps most importantly, I grew up in a highly dysfunctional family.

If you don't know what an ACE (Adverse Childhood Experiences) score is, it's a number that measures the types of childhood trauma one experienced before the age of 18[1] (see

1

Appendix A to calculate your own ACE score). My score is a 4, a score held by a little over 12.5% of the population. What does that 4 mean? Well, it's considered a pretty high score, which surprised me when I found out, since I really didn't think my family was that different from many other families. I was well cared for and I was never sexually abused in any way. I suppose that's why discovering that a 4 was a high score surprised me.

The scary thing is, according to the research, as your ACE score increases, so too do your risks of encountering other issues like health problems (physical and mental) and substance abuse. Plus, people with higher ACE scores tend to be less successful and struggle with their finances[2].

So how have I been able to achieve so much with such a high ACE score? How have I managed to avoid alcoholism and drug abuse? How was I able to become an adult with even a modicum of success?

How did I learn how to bounce back? How did I learn how to thrive, even when I was programmed (in many ways) to fail? I believe it is through the REBOUNDS Program, which is the result of my experience of going through setback after setback in life, fighting my way through, rebounding again and again, bouncing back and achieving my goals, in spite of some of the challenges life dealt to me.

The REBOUNDS Program takes into account that you too may have been programmed in very specific ways to fail. It takes into account the messages you heard growing up and the things you've been told as an adult. But it's much more than that.

This program, at its core, is about accepting that each of us has been given challenges in one way or another, but we are not defined solely by our challenges. You are not your ACE score. And you are far more resilient than you may imagine. Resilience is one of the biggest keys to conquering your ACE score, by the way (calculate your resilience score in Appendix B).

In addition to the challenges life brings, all of us have also been given gifts. Now is the time to recognize those gifts, own them, inhabit them, and fully realize your own potential.

You've probably been through a lot, or else you wouldn't be reading this book. Right now, you may feel like you can't do much more than just getting up each morning. That's okay. You don't have to do anything you don't want to do.

But make no mistake about it, I'm going to push you to do a *little* more than you think you can handle, a little faster than you think you can. *I* believe in you. I know that you can bounce back. I know that whatever has happened, you can bounce your way back to achieving everything you want in life.

My mom's favorite character in *Winnie the Pooh* was Tigger. I never asked her why, but looking back now, I think she loved Tigger's effervescent optimism. Tigger was the consummate BounceBack Artist. No matter what the trouble was, Tigger was ready to bounce that trouble away.

I want you to begin today by thinking of yourself as a little bit like Tigger. You're going to bounce your way back! You're going to rebound! You're going to get your mojo back!

And you're going to do it faster than you thought you could. The REBOUNDS Program is all about moving you out of this place of anger, frustration, depression, and resentment, and into a place of empowerment, achievement, and joy.

So let's jump in...or better yet, let's bounce!

> *"Buddy, if you're gonna pounce,*
> *you've got to have some bounce!"*
>
> - Tigger

Introduction

LIFE. IT'S A ROLLER coaster, isn't it? Things are going along well, everything's in harmony, you're happy and healthy, then BOOM. A setback. It's just how things are. From breakups and divorce to illness to lost clients and bad performance reviews, from the jobs you didn't get to the jobs you wish you hadn't, life is full of setbacks.

No One Is Immune

None of us is immune to setbacks, either. 100% of people fail in one form or another, at some point in their lives. There's literally *no one* on this planet who hasn't had a setback.

Let's look at a few examples. According to the Small Business Association, 30% of businesses fail in the first two years of operation. Of those that are left, 50% fail in the first five years. And 66% fail in the first ten years[3]. That means only 23.1% of businesses succeed past their first ten years, and only 1% will achieve millionaire status.

The failure rate is staggering. A business failure can have a significant impact on your self-worth and your belief in your ability to be a successful entrepreneur. If you close one business, you may be afraid to open another. If you do start another business, you're likely to be plagued with self-doubt and fear, which hampers good decision-making.

There's more. Only 2% of athletes go on to be successful as professional athletes[4]. That's a 98% failure rate!

Half of all marriages fail[5]. That's factoring in first, second, third, etc. marriages, and of all different types. One study in England showed that a quarter of British people married their first love, which means the remaining 75% experienced at least one heartbreak. Whether a breakup or a divorce, there's no shortage of stories of people who have no idea what to do with their lives after their marriage or a significant relationship ends. It's a deep setback, and unless you do some serious work, you're likely to take the damage from each failed relationship into the next one, creating even bigger potential for problems.

None of us is immune to setbacks, either. 100% of people fail in one form or another, at some point in their lives. There's literally no one on this planet who hasn't had a setback.

And if you talk about jobs...well, just imagine how many people apply for one position and don't get the job. Now consider how many people are out there in the world who have gone on *many* interviews and still haven't found the job they want. Imagine the folks who *did* get the job, but hated it. We know that happens a *lot*, because more than 70% of workers report that they are not satisfied with their jobs[6].

Now let's say you're one of those people who got the job, and your company, like most, does annual performance reviews. Setting aside my personal opinions regarding the efficacy of performance reviews, let's talk about what happens

in these reviews. 22% of people tend to cry in their performance reviews[7]. Crying in a performance review suggests to
me that it's not a great review—can we agree on that, generally speaking?

Once you've had a negative performance review, typically
things don't improve. 67% of companies report an increase in
absenteeism, resignations, or both from employees who have
experienced a negative performance review[8]. *Some* people
might be motivated by a negative performance review, but the
research shows that most are not. In fact, following a negative
performance review, 37% of people start looking for another
job and 20% flat-out quit[9]. That's 57% of people who have
had a bad appraisal instantly start looking for a way out.

When you've had a bad performance review, you feel horrible. You didn't get the raise, the promotion, the good scores,
or the positive feedback. You're angry, embarrassed, and
humiliated, and you're likely scared your job is in jeopardy.
You're worried that you're not who you thought you were,
and you're worried that other people think poorly of you.

Then you begin to dislike your job, so your performance
is even more negatively affected. Consequently, if you have
a negative performance review, you're more likely to have
another negative performance review, creating a downward
spiral.

All of these types of experiences can lead you to integrate
the negative feedback you receive in the process, regardless
of what form it takes. And ultimately you can easily end up
with a poor self-image, a lack of confidence, and even anxiety
and depression.

No one is immune to setbacks. We've all experienced them. And while some of us seem to live a charmed life with few setbacks, some of us have had more than others. In fact, some people experience so many setbacks that they wonder, "Is this all there is? Will life always be like this?"

Setbacks Can Proliferate

The funny thing about setbacks is that they're like Tribbles, those fuzzy little aliens from Star Trek. Like Tribbles, setbacks can replicate like crazy. That's right, one setback, if not handled properly, can beget another, and another and another. In fact, that's why some people have experienced so many setbacks. Setbacks create their very own cascade effect.

There's Good News

Here's the good news; it doesn't have to be like that. Having spent the last 20 years working with clients on their setbacks and helping them bounce back, as well as bouncing back from my own setbacks, I devised a simple formula to help my clients bounce back from their setbacks - to turn them into BounceBack Artists. Note that I'm saying it's a *simple* formula. I'm *not* saying that it's *easy*. But it's eminently doable.

I grew up unconsciously knowing the BounceBack Artist formula. I used it every day, every time I dealt with trouble at home, when I experienced romantic breakups, any time someone said something unkind to me. The REBOUNDS Program has helped me through every bad moment, bad job, every setback I ever encountered—even The Great Recession. It's always been a part of who I am.

As a coach, in addition to a great big toolbox of coaching tools, I apply the strategies that have been successful in my own life to my client work, helping clients bounce back from failing businesses, bad relationships and breakups, bad interviews and jobs lost, and those dreaded bad job performance reviews.

My clients, who hired me feeling lost, frustrated, angry, pessimistic about the future, or generally unsure of where to turn next, <u>all</u> rebounded and relaunched, finding themselves back in their lives, happier and more fulfilled than ever. In this book I'll share some of their stories with you[1]. The truth is, it took a while for them to bounce back, and in the last couple of years, I started to wonder, "Is it possible to rebound faster? Does it *have* to take so long?"

The answer, as I discovered, is *no.* You don't have to take a year or more to rebound from a setback. You can bounce back and relaunch in just nine weeks. And that's exactly what we're going to do.

You don't have to take a year or more to rebound from a setback. You can bounce back and relaunch in just nine weeks.

---

1 All names and identifying details have been changed to protect my clients' privacy and confidentiality. Most stories are composites of multiple clients.

[1]

"If Only I'd Done the Work Sooner"

I'LL NEVER FORGET THE first person who called me crying, because she'd had a bad job performance review. Joanne was a successful executive who'd worked hard, played the game, and thought she'd done everything it took...until her review came, and she was blindsided when her boss told her she hadn't been meeting expectations.

Setting aside the fact that with good leadership strategies, feedback like this should *never* come as a surprise, Joanne was devastated. She was in shock, most of all. She'd worked hard and thought she was meeting important benchmarks, so when she heard, "not meeting expectations," her stomach dropped, and she actually stopped hearing anything else.

She didn't hear the good things her boss was pleased with. She didn't hear him tell her how she could improve. She couldn't focus on the advice he offered. All she could do was sit there and try not to cry.

When Joanne called me, she said, "I feel helpless. I had no idea this was coming, and I can't believe I didn't see it."

It had been several weeks since the review. In that time, she had ruminated over the conversation so many times that she was completely defeated, beaten down, and she had no idea how to move on. She didn't even feel as if she *could* move on.

"I'm desperate," she told me, "I used to love my job, and now I hate it. I sit in meetings resenting everyone and everything. I can't stop thinking about what my boss said to me, and I'm terrified that all my coworkers know what happened. I'm humiliated."

Joanne was in pain. Her whole world had come crashing down around her, all because of some negative feedback from her boss. When I asked her what positive things he'd said, she was unable to recall anything good that had come out of the review (more on why her memory worked that way later!)

She told me she'd taken some time off work to deal with her emotions and figure out next steps. It hadn't worked. She returned to work and was just as miserable as she had been before she left. She couldn't get back into the swing of things, once she believed her boss thought so little of her.

Joanne's experience wasn't unusual. Not by a long shot. It's not at all uncommon for people to react like this to a negative performance review, especially when it comes as a huge shock.

Most people are unprepared for the shock and have no idea how to handle the situation. They're angry, hurt, embarrassed, shamed, terrified their coworkers will know, and fearful of losing their livelihoods. And they think they can't possibly return to a state of equilibrium at their current job, which is why so many people end up checking out at work or eventually, leaving their jobs. In fact, that's exactly what Joanne did. After we spoke, she took some time to think about what she wanted to do. Eventually, Joanne decided that her boss was wrong, her company was the worst, and, rather than working with a coach, she would just find another job where they *did* appreciate her.

> *Most people are unprepared for the shock and have no idea how to handle the situation. They're angry, hurt, embarrassed, shamed, terrified their coworkers will know, and fearful of losing their livelihoods.*

Joanne went to work for another company. This time, though, she started out with a chip on her shoulder and took the damage from the previous job into her new role. It didn't go well.

She called me a year later, after another bad performance review. Her psyche was even more broken and battered this time around, because she hadn't properly gone through the process of dealing with the first review.

This time, after all she'd been through, Joanne was finally ready to do the work. Super motivated, she completed the nine step REBOUNDS Program in twelve weeks. Twelve weeks! It took her just three months to navigate through and come out on the other side...and she could've done it so much sooner.

I always wondered how much angst, resentment, and stress she would have saved herself if she'd worked the process the first time...and so did she. In our last session together, she said, "If only I'd done the work sooner!"

[2]

THE BOUNCEBACK ARTIST IS BORN

WHEN I WAS IN college, I took a summer temp job working as the front office receptionist at a local radio station. I loved it. I was the first face everyone saw when they walked into the building, and I could see the DJ booth right from my desk. I worked hard at that job, and I thrived in the fast-paced environment. I did so well that when Julie, the station's executive assistant, was going out on maternity leave, she recommended me to take her place temporarily.

I was so excited to take on the new challenge. Julie supported all of the salespeople who sold advertising on the radio station, as well as the sales manager and the general manager of the station. I dove into the job, just as I had the receptionist job. The executive assistant job was very different from the receptionist job. When I was working at the front desk, I just had to answer the phone, give directions, and make coffee and copies. I didn't have a ton of direct contact with the salespeople or anyone else who worked at the station, except when they were coming and going. Even then, few of them came through the front door—our staff parking lot was in the back. I had very little contact with the staff until I was working in that back office, supporting them directly.

Before that summer, I had really only worked two jobs. I had worked retail, but my first job was working for my dad in his medical practice. I had worked for him since I was 13 years old, and over the years had picked up some of his habits in the professional workplace. At times my dad has a caustic and sarcastic sense of humor, and I must have picked that up and brought it into *my* workplace, because it wasn't too long before I was called into the sales manager's office for a meeting.

The sales manager told me that some of the staff said I had been rude to them, when I was supposed to be supportive and helpful. He said, "You were so pleasant at the front desk, I can't imagine why that changed, but you can't treat your co-workers like that.." He also told me I had to straighten up and remember that I was there to help the sales team. He reminded me that I worked *for* them, not exactly *with* them.

I was horrified. *Horrified.* I thought I had been doing a really good job! I could not believe that my jokes had been so horribly misunderstood. And who ratted me out, anyway? I was so angry at whomever it was that complained about me. And I was terribly embarrassed. I wanted to disappear into the floor.

I remember how red my face felt. You know that feeling when your face is hot and just *feels* red? My face was burning. I remember crying. I felt so much shame and embarrassment, thinking about how I had let everyone down and that I hadn't lived up to the potential they'd seen in me when they hired me.

I was so ashamed. I didn't want anyone to know that I had been told off, but I assumed *everyone* knew.

I went to the bathroom and hid in the stall for awhile. I didn't want anyone to see that I had been crying. I also didn't want to go back to my desk. At all. I wanted to get in my car and drive away and never come back.

But I didn't do that. I couldn't. I was a broke college student and I was being paid by the hour: I needed the money.

I wiped away my tears and went back to my desk. For the rest of that day, I tried to pretend I was Julie, the regular executive assistant, and do everything the way she would have done it. I couldn't make eye contact with anyone. I couldn't laugh or chat the way I normally would have. I was devastated.

I went home and cried and ate ice cream. It was my first big career setback - the first time someone told me, "You are not doing a good job right now."

I wanted to stay home the next day and cry some more, but I had to work. So I did.

That day, I tried to be nice to everyone and I also tried to be deferential. I still felt horribly ashamed and embarrassed, but I also realized that I really liked my job and wanted to keep it as long as I could. I even had secret hopes that Julie would like being a mom so much that maybe she wouldn't want to come back to her job.

It took awhile for me to feel okay again. I didn't know it then, but I was in the midst of my very first bounceback.

It's easier to rebound from something like this when you're a college student and have less to lose. While I liked my job and wanted to keep it, the truth is, I didn't earn much money back then, and if I lost that job, another relatively low-paying job would have been available. I could've gone back to work for my dad, or I could've taken a job at a pizza place or worked fast food. I had options.

Working at that radio station wasn't the same as the jobs (and business) I would have down the road. Back then, I didn't have my entire career on the line, and my livelihood wasn't exactly at stake. As a result, bouncing back was easier.

If you've experienced a setback that's shaken you to your core, then it doesn't actually matter if it's the first or the twentieth.

Still, I look back at that time as the time when the Bounce-Back Artist and the REBOUNDS Program were born. It was the first time I had ever experienced a blow like that, and it wouldn't be the last.

I rebounded so well that when I left the radio station (Julie did come back, by the way), I had glowing letters of recommendation from the general manager and the sales manager, talking about my pleasant personality and what an asset I would make to any team. Every member of the sales team came to my goodbye party and wished me well. When I joined LinkedIn over 20 years later and happened upon that sales manager, he actually remembered me from all those years before.

So what made that first bounceback relatively easy? The truth is, all first setbacks aren't so easy. Sometimes the first one is the hardest, because you're forced to face a painful reality: everyone in the world doesn't think you're as amazing as your mom does. For some, that realization can come as a big shock.

On the other hand, the first setback can be easy to rebound from, because you're only rebounding from that one thing. Subsequent setbacks may be harder, because you most likely haven't fully processed the damage to your psyche from previous setbacks, and that damage can really stack up.

It's also much easier to rebound when you don't have much at stake. If you're reading this, you've probably experienced a setback and have a lot to lose. If you've experienced a setback that's shaken you to your core, then it doesn't actually matter if it's the first or the twentieth.

Every rebound starts with you getting out of your own way. Nothing will change unless you decide that you are ready to change.

What's most important about rebounding and relaunching is the philosophy that's at the very heart of the REBOUNDS Program: that *every rebound starts with you getting out of your own way.* **Nothing will change unless you decide that *you* are ready to change.**

This is true even if you work in a toxic culture. This is true if you had an unfair review. This is true if you got "storied" (this is when a manager chooses an employee, crafts a negative narrative around that person, so that s/he can "help" the employee to improve, and thus, the manager looks good in the process—it's always a losing game for the employee, though). It's true if you're going through a bad breakup or a divorce. It's true if life dealt you a horrible hand.

No matter what you've gone through, no matter what the setback, nothing will change until you are ready to get out of your own way and change, evolve, and grow.

[3]

THE SECOND SETBACK

MY SECOND TIME AROUND the setback block wasn't so easy. I went through breakups, sure, and of course personal, romantic entanglements are always challenging to rebound from, but my next *major* setback was also career-related. I'd been working for a university and was recruited by a magazine publishing company. During the job interview, I was completely captivated by the position, the company, the fact that they brought in fresh fruit every day (back when that was a big deal) and their big promises to hire an assistant for me within a year. It was my first real corporate job.

I started that job with so much enthusiasm and confidence. The Internet was still new, my web development skills were in demand, and I was super excited that a company wanted *me*.

Within two weeks of working my new job, I knew there was a problem. The only other woman on my team was in charge of managing our web servers, and she started checking my code.

Now, if you're not technical, that's okay. Just know that there is a bit of an art to coding. Everyone who codes has their own style, just like with writing. Some people are extremely concise in their code. Some like a lot of documentation in the code, some are beautifully eloquent. There's more than one right way to code. While some ways are better and more efficient than others, what really matters is that the code works and can be picked up and understood by someone else who might come along after you to work on the code.

My code worked well across browsers and platforms, exactly as it was supposed to. I preferred to keep my code clean, without much documentation, because frankly, it was simple, straightforward code that didn't *need* to be documented. My coworker felt differently. She liked documenting practically every line. She started emailing me. Every night. In the middle of the night. She'd send me one email for each thing she felt I hadn't done the way she would have done it. In each email, she would say that my code was wrong, when in fact, it was just not done the way she would do it.

At the university, I had been treated with respect. People trusted me and my code. I had taught web design and development to staff, faculty, and students. How could my code be *wrong*, when it was clean and most importantly, it *worked*?

At first I would come into work and check on the emails, then respond to all of them in one email, letting her know that my code was working.

But when she didn't get the result she wanted, she started cc'ing her emails to our boss, who knew nothing about code. Even though he knew she was a little nutty, she'd been working at the company longer, so he trusted her more. He told me just to deal with it. I know now that he wasn't a great boss, but back then I began to think something was wrong with me that I couldn't cope with this coworker and get her to leave me alone.

The emails got worse: capital letters and insults. Sometimes I would come into work to find thirty-five or forty emails in my inbox, written at two or three o'clock in the morning. Sometimes, upon hearing my arrival in my cubicle, this woman (who worked a couple of cubicles away) would come in and tell me she'd found problems in my code and sent me emails. I would politely thank her, explain I had just gotten in, and tell her I would look at them when I had a chance. If I didn't respond to the emails immediately, she would come back in and tell me how bad I was at my job, and how I was wrong that there were different coding styles.

Finally, I went to the Human Resources Department. They looked at the email trail and decided that she was stalking me, and they made her go to therapy. Still, things did not improve. My stress levels continued to increase, and I frequently went home and cried.

Anyone who knows me knows that I have a terrible memory. But one of my clearest memories of this time in my life was when I took a beach vacation, hoping to recuperate from some of the stress. I sat in my beachfront condo staring at the ocean and crying my eyes out for an entire week. When I got home, I felt exactly the same as I had when I left. And I still had to go back to that job.

Back then, just as now, I was resourceful. I bought and read tons of books on how to handle a difficult coworker. I talked to friends, colleagues, and even sought counseling. None of the advice worked. Nothing helped. I began to worry that maybe this woman was right about my code, and waged a battle within myself, debating what I *knew* to be true against what I was being told about my work.

Then, one day, I had a performance review. My boss told me that he had heard that I was difficult and that I wasn't following my coworker's instructions regarding my coding. I was shocked.

I argued with him. I defended myself. I reminded him what he had told me about "dealing with it" and explained what I had been putting up with. I asked if he had given my coworker a bad review as well. I told him it wasn't fair.

In short, if you've ever read an article of any substance on how to handle yourself in a performance review, I did the exact opposite of what you're supposed to do.

After that review, I became so angry, so frustrated, so resentful, that I started not to care - about my job, about my work. I hated my job. I hated my boss. I hated my coworker. And I hated the injustice of it all.

I developed carpal tunnel syndrome, a repetitive stress injury in the forearms and wrists that happens frequently to coders (and writers); I, of course, attributed it to having to reply to so many emails.

Carpal tunnel syndrome became my way out. I filed a worker's compensation claim and eventually, quit my job. I was so damaged and hurt by the experience that I never went back to working for anyone else again (which, side note, has turned out to be a really good thing after all).

It took years for me to get over what happened at that job. I went to therapy and talked about it a lot. I still felt angry. I worked with several coaches in those years, and I always felt like the platitudes they offered to inspire me were useless.

They would suggest that I needed to be optimistic. They told me to have faith. They told me to "get back in the game and try again." When I got stuck in the story of what had happened to me, no one knew how to help me move on.

Not one therapist, counselor, or coach suggested that I do what I'm going to suggest to you in these pages. In fact, it wasn't until I began to think about my previous life experience and how I had conquered my setbacks before that I rediscovered REBOUNDS and put it to work again for myself.

Not one therapist, counselor, or coach suggested that I do what I'm going to suggest to you in these pages.

[4]

PUTTING REBOUNDS BACK INTO PLACE

ONCE I REMEMBERED HOW I had once gotten myself over the hump of a setback and rebounded, I tried to try to diagram out how I did it. At this point, I had started my coaching career, and I was curious about what I could glean from my own past success in conquering a big hurdle.

I realized that it wasn't just feeling my anger, but *processing* it that started my rebound journey. I had to look carefully at *why* I was so hurt and angry, *why* I felt embarrassed and humiliated. I had to get down in the muck and get dirty with my ugly, unprocessed feelings, and begin to *understand* them.

Then I had to let those ugly feelings go and move on. Just as, back at that radio station, I had to look at and critically assess the feedback I'd been given, I had to look back on the feedback I received at my job. I had to consider what I was told and assess it with complete honesty and integrity.

Once I decided not to tell myself any more stories about my past, but rather, to face the past with absolute honesty, I was able to sort out the stalking behavior of my colleague from the feedback. I could suddenly see that, while I didn't have to tolerate her bad behavior, I had more to learn than I realized back then. I could have been more open to her feedback, and treated her with more respect.

I also began to see how my behavior changed when she challenged my code and the quality of my work. I realized that she had touched a deep wound that I didn't know was there, a wound that constantly told me, "You're not good enough." That's why her criticism hurt me so deeply.

I want to be clear that I'm not saying that my coworker was right in bullying and stalking me. Far from it. **Because I was able to separate her bad behavior from the message she was actually trying to communicate, I could see clearly where my responsibility was and how I might have handled myself more effectively in the situation.**

I was also able to see what I needed to work on so that I never found myself in a situation like that again. Back then, while I was very happy in my new coaching practice, I wasn't sure what the future might hold. I wanted to be prepared, just in case I wanted or needed to go back to the corporate world someday.

I faced myself and my own demons through the RE-BOUNDS process (it had no name back then, it was just an idea I was trying, really). Not only did I heal myself from the damage I suffered, but I learned a tremendous amount about myself and who I was capable of being...and I became the best version of myself.

REBOUNDS was just being born back then. Since that time, I've honed it, tested it, honed it more, and tested some more. What you're holding in your hands represents more than two decades of work. And it's the most effective strategy for bouncing back from setbacks that has ever been created.

***REBOUNDS** is the most effective strategy for bouncing back from setbacks that has ever been created.*

[5]

WHAT HAPPENS DURING REBOUNDS?

I'D BEEN PUTTING THE REBOUNDS Program into place, testing it with clients, honing it and improving it. Then a client, Marie, came to me and said, "I love the idea of this program, but I can't wait. I only have a six month window to show my bosses I can change, and if I don't, I'm losing my job. I'm miserable and I don't want to do it, but I can't afford to lose this job now."

I put the program on fast-forward for Marie. In six months, she was able to turn things around completely, and her bosses were amazed at the transformation.

Marie's rebound went so well that I wanted to see what else was possible. Could it be done in 12 weeks? Could it be done in six?

I experimented. I tried different methods. Some strategies worked better when they were sped up. Some didn't. After testing the method again and again, I finally settled on nine weeks. Nine weeks to transform your life, get your spring back in your step, and relaunch yourself as a rock star.

Now, just to be clear, it isn't just nine weeks and you're done. The nine weeks is the bulk of the program. After you complete the program, you'll enter the Maintenance phase, where you'll lock in everything you've done in the first nine weeks.

> *Now, just to be clear, it isn't just nine weeks and you're done.*

Changing Your Brain

There are a lot of ideas about what it takes to change our brains. The idea that it takes 30 days to change a habit is often repeated by coaches. They support their claim by talking about a NASA experiment designed to assess how astronauts cope with some of the disorientation in space. The story goes that for 24 hours a day, 7 days a week, astronauts were required to wear special glasses that made everything they looked at appear upside down. Somewhere between Day 26 and Day 30, the astronauts' brains adjusted, so that they began to see everything right-side up again, all while wearing the glasses.

However, this study with these results never actually happened. Other studies did happen[10], but somehow this particular legend has been taken as fact, and many coaches have extrapolated from that story to suggest that our brains can rewire themselves at around 30 days. But the problem is, while our brains might very well rewire themselves at 30 days, it doesn't mean we've created a new habit.

Newer research indicates it can take up to 6 months to create a new habit or way of thinking and really lock it in[11]. So instead of looking for the fast fix, brace yourself: you're in for nine weeks of intense work, plus another four months of staying on track and locking that work in.

The great news, though, is that this work is uplifting work. It's positive work.

Let me tell you about Angela, an executive who called me, desperate, three months after she'd bombed a job interview. It was a job she *really* wanted, and she was kicking herself all over the place for not having gotten it. The recruiter had told her all of the reasons why they didn't give her the job, and that feedback had not only paralyzed her, but it had made her afraid to go into any other interviews. Not only that, but Angela was completely disengaged at her current job, and it was also affecting her relationship with her husband, because all she could talk about was how miserable she was.

Angela and I spoke on the phone. I listened to her breaking down, talking about her frustration with herself, her self-doubt, and how discouraged she felt. When she had shared everything, and I knew the REBOUNDS Program was right for her, I laid out the steps and explained how it worked.

Sometimes just making a decision to take action toward a rebound makes a big difference in how you feel. Angela told me later that by the end of that conversation she felt as if a burden had been lifted. She said, "For months I had talked to friends, I had talked to coworkers, and no one had made me see the future in such a positive light. After I talked to you, **I felt hope for the first time in ages.**"

Angela took the first steps and joined the program, and over the next nine weeks, diligently completed her home-work, doing everything I asked of her.

As she progressed through the program, she found her spirits continued to rise. Her relationship with her husband improved dramatically. She began to re-engage at work, impressing her boss so much that within a year, he offered her a promotion that was far better than any of the jobs she'd been interviewing for.

The REBOUNDS Program helped Angela to get her life back *and then some.* She found her confidence and self-worth, discovered how and why she'd been holding herself back (for years!), and uncovered more power within herself than she had ever imagined possible.

The REBOUNDS Program can help you, too. If you follow the steps I outline, then you can bounce back from just about any setback you've experienced and achieve all the things you've imagined.

Brace yourself—you're about to bounce back!

[6]

THE **REBOUNDS** PROGRAM

THE REBOUNDS PROGRAM IS comprised of eight steps, and it's designed to be worked for at least nine weeks (this will make sense shortly). Now...before I outline the program clearly for you, I want to be fully candid with you about this program and the time it takes to go through it.

When I say it takes nine weeks, that's *on average.* The reality is that if you're super "gung ho" and raring to go, if you're motivated and ready to jump in with both feet and do every step of this program, working the program every single day, then you *can* complete it in nine weeks. I've had clients who were able to accomplish this goal without any problem.

Everyone's different. You may need to take a little more time in some of the steps than others. That's okay. The goal isn't to hold yourself to some deadline that I created for you. The goal is to keep your foot on the gas, but stop when you see stop signs. If your gut tells you to take your time with one of the steps, then slow down for it. Just be cautious about it, and remain self-aware.

One of the challenges of working a program from a book, instead of having a coach like me right there beside you as you work through the program, is that you don't have me there to give you a gentle nudge when I think you're unconsciously holding yourself back (though you *can* have me there—just flip to the back of the book to find out how). If you're doing this on your own, you'll have to stay hyper-aware of your own intentions. When you sense yourself taking more time than you absolutely need one of the steps, you'll need to put some pressure on yourself to move

> *Everyone's different. You may need to take a little more time in some of the steps than others. That's okay.*

forward. Similarly, if you think you're moving too fast, it's okay to slow yourself down and give yourself a chance to breathe and think and process.

The REBOUNDS Program is designed to move you out of resentment, frustration, anger, and fear, and into a place of empowerment and joy. And while most of my examples will be related to jobs, interviews, performance reviews, and career, you can easily apply the REBOUNDS Program to *any* setback in your life.

These eight steps will help you whether you've had a bad performance evaluation at work, you're going through a divorce, or you've let yourself get out of shape and unhealthy. Heck, these eight steps helped me bounce back recently, when I discovered that I was in early menopause and would never have my own children—which may have been my biggest and most significant rebound to date (and certainly took more than nine weeks).

In this chapter, I'll outline the eight steps. In subsequent chapters, I'll give more detail for each step. Again, generally, it's one week per step, but you can take a little more time if you need to, just be sure not to linger for too long on any one step.

One last thing before I jump into outlining the program: If you're experiencing mental illness, profound anxiety or depression, if you're enmeshed in a toxic or abusive relationship, or you're involved with drug or alcohol abuse, please seek help. In any of these situations, please do not embark upon this program without first consulting a therapist. **If you're experiencing any suicidal thoughts, please call the National Suicide Prevention Lifeline at 1-800-273-8255.** They can help you to stop feeling so much pain, and they can get you the help you need.

THE REBOUNDS PROGRAM

STEP 1: REVEL IN THE PAIN, THEN EXPEL IT

We begin REBOUNDS by encouraging you to let yourself feel the anger, resentment, sadness, all the "junk" emotions. In Step 1, it's okay to feel bad (this is one of the reasons that it's *not* a good idea for profoundly depressed people to embark upon this program without the supervision and assistance of a qualified therapist. If you're severely depressed, the *last* thing you should be doing is adding to the pain you already feel).

For the rest of you, you're going to get down in the dirt and wallow in it. I want you to *really* wallow. Like, swim in it.

In the next chapter, I'll explain why this step is so important and why it's the first step in the program.

In the second part of Step 1, you're going to let go of all the pain from the first part. You'll release all the junk from the past, and start to look toward the future. You're going to gain clarity on where you're going. The future is like the destination on a GPS, and the GPS won't let you do anything until you've set it. You're going to set that destination so you know where you're heading.

Since there are two parts to Step 1, you'll want to plan for two weeks (at least) for this step.

STEP 2: EVALUATE THE FEEDBACK

In Step 2, you're going to clearly and honestly take stock of where you are now. What you're doing in this step is akin to setting the "Current Location" area on the GPS. You're also going to assess any feedback you've been given—in a job interview, from a loved one, during a performance review, from your doctor—and consider which pieces of that feedback need to be kept, and which ones can be discarded.

STEP 3: BUILD A PLAN

In Step 3, you're going to determine which changes you want to make, as you integrate the feedback you decided to keep in Step 2. You'll create a plan to make real changes—*exactly* how you're going to evolve and grow—and you're going to commit to making those changes. This step is difficult, but it's not the hardest step. That's coming up next!

STEP 4: OVERHAUL YOURSELF

In Step 4, you're going to start implementing the changes you committed to in Step 3. *This* is where things actually get pretty serious. In fact, this is where most people give up. I help you to be prepared to avoid the common reasons why people quit during this step.

STEP 5: UNDERSTAND RESISTANCE

Step 5 is where you'll respond to resistance to the changes you're going to be making. There are two types of resistance you'll have to respond to: internal and external. I'll give you strategies to handle both of them.

STEP 6: NOTIFY IMPORTANT PEOPLE

Step 6 is where you're going to become *visible* to the people who matter. If you're going to relaunch yourself at work, for example, then you'll want your bosses to know what you're up to. We'll talk about to whom you want to make yourself known and how to make yourself known to them.

STEP 7: DENY RESISTANCE

I'll bet you thought you took care of all the resistance in Step 5. Nope. Resistance comes up a few times as we make changes in our lives. I want you to be prepared for it, because resistance can keep you from achieving your goals.

Whether it's a little voice in your head causing self-doubt, a family member discouraging you, or a well-meaning friend who just doesn't understand, resistance can be extraordinarily strong. That's why you're going to be equipped to respond powerfully to it.

STEP 8: SOAR!

The last step is your official relaunch: the relaunch of the new you, a time when you'll begin to soar again. Most of this section is about cleaning house and clearing the way for the new you. In reality, you've been relaunching this whole time. But in Step 8, we're going to talk about how to make sure your rebound gets locked in...and we'll talk about what to do in the next few months as well.

The eight steps may seem simple on the surface. But make no mistake about it, these steps are fraught with pitfalls and challenges. In subsequent chapters, I'll give you clear guidance for what to do next and what to expect. I'll also share common places where you may get stuck, and what to do when that happens.

BEFORE YOU JUMP IN...

One last thing. When I first start working with a client, *before* I begin to challenge them, I encourage them to come up with strategies for how they'll get unstuck when things get sticky. It's not just about the guidance I give you, but how motivated you are to make this bounceback happen.

Right now, ask yourself how important this is to you. Ask yourself if you're prepared to stay with the process when things get hard, when you're struggling, when you're not feeling motivated, and when you think something I'm suggesting doesn't make sense or you think it's dumb. Are you prepared to stay in this game with me? I'll stay in it with you, but you have to stay in it for yourself to see a real bounceback happen.

More than that, I want you to start thinking *now* about what happens when you get stuck and what you'll do to get yourself unstuck. Laying the foundation of those plans now is a lot easier than doing it when you actually are stuck and are experiencing the brain junk and desperation that comes with being stuck. Part of getting stuck is feeling a lack of resources, which is all perception and rarely truth. If you set out a plan *now*, so that you can access your resources *then*, at a time when you feel like you have the least resources, then you'll be better prepared to find your way out of the "stuckness."

Remember, I'm here for you. I'm just an email away, so count me among your resources. You can get in touch with me by going to BounceBackArtist.com/contact, and I encourage you to let me know how you're doing!

Now, get to work!

[7]

STEP ONE, PART ONE: REVEL IN THE PAIN

CHANCES ARE THAT JUST picking up this book already made you feel better. When we perceive ourselves as "in action" toward a resolution of a problem, we automatically begin to feel better. Brace yourself: this feeling is temporary. It's an illusion. All you've done is pick up a book. You haven't started to make any changes yet.

The changes begin with you accepting what's happened. Whatever the setback is, it's time to acknowledge the entire experience and the feelings that came with it.

Again, please remember that if you are experiencing any form of mental illness, including anxiety and particularly depression, you should consult with a therapist before embarking upon the REBOUNDS Program. The first step is a big one, and it does involve purposefully allowing yourself to feel the weight of all the emotions that came with your setback.

I cannot emphasize this enough - **if you have any suicidal thoughts, please call the National Suicide Prevention Lifeline at 1-800-273-8255.** They can help you immediately, and at that point, a therapist will be a much better fit for you right now. If you are in that head space, this is *not* the right program for you.

STEP ONE, PART ONE: REVEL IN THE PAIN

The first part of the first step of the REBOUNDS Program is to Revel in the Pain. Let the wave of emotions crash over you. I also call it "feeling the bad." All too often we push away negative, painful emotions, in the hopes that they'll just go away. Pain hurts. We don't want to feel that pain, right? So we push it away.

> *Whatever the setback is, it's time to acknowledge the entire experience and the feelings that came with it.*

THE PROBLEM WITH PUSHING AWAY THE PAIN

Pushing the pain away means you're avoiding it, and that's a short-term solution. It never actually works long-term. Eventually, you have to deal with those feelings. Not doing so can have pretty serious consequences.

One such consequence is that the feelings will come back, and sometimes they'll come back at an inappropriate or inopportune time. Sometimes they'll come back bigger than they were before.

If you don't deal with your feelings now, you'll leave yourself with an open wound, and in the future, it's quite possible that someone could inadvertently poke that wound, and your reaction could be much larger than necessary, simply because you never dealt with the feelings in a timely manner.

Keeping your feelings at bay can also lead to mental health challenges like anxiety and depression. You can become overwhelmed, overly angry, and irritable, and being in this state can impact your relationships.

Another consequence of not dealing with bad feelings can be the toll it can take on your physical health. When you don't let yourself experience and process your feelings, your body can suffer. We carry tension in our bodies a *lot* so you can really notice it in your muscles, if you pay attention. (There's a great book about this subject by a Welsh author named Kyle Davies, called *The Intelligent Body*, if you want to learn more about this phenomenon.)

> *When you don't let yourself experience and process your feelings, your body can suffer.*

Right now, take a moment to do a body scan. Where are you holding tension? Do you feel it in your back? Your neck? It's not uncommon to find specific places in your body where you carry stress. We're all a little different and we each carry stress a little differently. Try and relax the part of your body that is carrying the most stress right now, and see how you feel.

It's more than just tension (although that *should* be enough - carrying that kind of tension can lead to headaches, migraines, and other kinds of pain in the body), though. Carrying stress also can lead to stomach trouble, rising blood pressure, and many other health problems. Your body will make sure you're aware of what you're doing, too.

Many years ago, I found out that I had rosacea, a skin condition that makes my face (particularly my nose) turn red when I experience stress (or eat spicy food or drink red wine). My doctor gave me a cream and it helped some. A few years after that, I found out that I had gastritis, a chronic inflammation of the stomach lining that's often exacerbated by stress, spicy food, and alcohol. My doctor gave me some medicine and it helped.

There was a point at which I thought, "Hey, wait, why are these things happening to me? Is it possible that my body wants me to avoid stress, spicy food, and wine?" *Gee, you think?*

I began to make active changes to the way I handled my emotions and stress, and *both* conditions improved dramatically. What a surprise, right?

When I changed my eating and exercise habits as well, both conditions all but disappeared. I even slept better. These days, when I indulge a little in a glass of wine with dinner or an occasional gin and tonic, neither my tummy nor my face flares up, because I've been taking care of myself in other ways, managing my stress. But if I slip on taking care of my stress, oh boy, does my body let me know!

Stress has a *huge* impact on the body and the mind, and ignoring and pushing away bad feelings caused by setbacks is one surefire way to cause yourself a lot of trouble and potentially risk your health.

In this first week, you're going to let yourself feel all the bad feelings. That's it. It's pretty simple. When you start feeling better, remind yourself, "Nope, I'm supposed to be feeling bad this week," and try remembering all the elements of the setback that caused you to pick up this book in the first place. Relive the setback and let yourself feel the bad. Wallow in it. Seriously.

BE WILLING TO SIT WITH YOUR PAIN

You might be tempted to skip this first step, but please don't. You need to let yourself feel the feelings completely and fully. It isn't going to be an easy week. You might be sad, angry, frustrated, resentful, or a whole host of other emotions that we typically consider "negative." But these emotions exist for a reason, and they're not there to be ignored and pushed away.

> *You might be tempted to skip this first step, but please don't. You need to let yourself feel the feelings completely and fully.*

Really get into this step. Cry in the shower. Punch your pillow. Be angry.

We are often tempted to push away the pain or do things to distract ourselves from it. I encourage you to sit with it and discover that it does not kill you to do so.

Pema Chödrön, an American Tibetan Buddhist, wrote, "Can I touch the center of my pain? Can I sit with suffering, both yours and mine, without trying to make it go away? Can I stay present to the ache of loss or disgrace—disappointment in all its many forms—and let it open me?[12]"

I want you to sit with your suffering without trying to make it go away. Feel all your feelings. Don't push them away. Stay present and let yourself touch the center of your pain.

If you can, journal about your pain. Journaling is an important part of this first step. Tell your story, get it out on paper (or screen) and talk about what you experienced and how angry you feel. Feel the pain and write about it. Identify the pain and its causes. Where does it come from? Dig deep here, because it doesn't *only* come from the things that have happened, it also comes from your interpretation of what happened and the causes. This pain comes from a deeper source. Try to find that source.

If you're not a writer, then talk to a recording device, use voice recognition software, or talk to your camera on your phone instead, so that at least you have something that you can look back at later in the steps.

A FEW CAUTIONARY NOTES:

Do *not* take these feelings out on your loved ones, and don't exhibit them at work. That's not the point of this exercise and exhibiting them in front of others will not be particularly conducive to the work we're doing here. The point is that you need to *feel* these feelings, not necessarily *show* them.

No escaping! Try not to numb yourself against the pain. Typically we avoid our feelings by drinking too much, watching too much TV, eating comfort foods, or getting absorbed in our phones and other devices. Try not to do those things. *You need to let yourself feel it all so that you can process it, so that you can acknowledge it and begin to fix it.*

PROCESSING

During this time, I also want you to think about your feelings and analyze them. Why do you feel the way that you do? Are there specific things that triggered these feelings, and do the feelings you're having remind you of any other times in your life?

Are the feelings familiar to you? Have you ever felt them before? If so, when? What was happening at the time that you felt these feelings before?

It's okay if you can't make sense of all of your feelings. They don't have to make sense now...or at all. However, if you can, try to assess which ones are the biggest ones, and get more specific with what those feelings are and where they came from.

Making sense of your feelings can be tricky when you're going it alone. Having a coach or therapist by your side to help you work through them is almost always beneficial. When you're working through this process on your own, you won't have the benefit of someone giving you an outside perspective and thinking of things and noticing cues that you might not think of or be aware of.

I can't count the number of times that clients have said, "I never would have thought of that!" or who have experienced a major mindset shift after talking through their feelings, simply because I saw something they couldn't see.

The coaching relationship is like a painting. In your life, you're *in* the painting. You can't always see the big, full picture. You can't see the frame. You can only see the image close up. However, someone who's standing in a museum or gallery looking at your picture? They can see everything, and they can see things that you simply can't see. That's why a coach is so valuable to this process. I can see things you can't.

Your goal is to understand your feelings as best you can. You'll be able to do a fair amount on your own.

Having said that, your goal is to understand your feelings as best you can, and you'll be able to do a fair amount on your own. Don't push the feelings away. Let yourself feel them and begin to process them.

RUMINATING

You'll want to be aware of *rumination,* one of the likely causes of people getting stuck in their feelings. Ruminating is when you think about something over and over and over, turning it this way and that, analyzing repetitively. Ruminating is rarely useful. In fact, it's a fruitless exercise.

You may feel compelled to go over the things that happened, conversations you had, feedback you received, comments that people made and question whether you responded the "right" way. You may want to think about whether you missed something in this conversation or that one. There are *many* kinds of ruminating, none of it helpful to the cause of understanding what happened and why.

We think that ruminating will help us to uncover some hidden truth. That's why we do it. "If I just think about this thing long enough, I'll get to the bottom of it," we believe. We also ruminate, our brains cycling through our negative experiences again and again, because our brains are hardwired to negativity. It's literally easier for our brains to go to the negative than to the positive. Negativity exerts a stronger pull on us than positivity does.

Many of my clients have been "expert ruminators," and it's an easy habit to fall into, especially for women. One of my clients took notes in a performance review and every morning after the review, she would pull out her notes and remind herself of all of the negative feedback she'd received. She didn't write down the good feedback. Every morning, she relived the negative parts of that review, and reminded herself of her failings, going over everything she had said and done and trying to find the answers to why she had gotten such a bad review.

Another client kept negative feedback for years, locked away in a filing cabinet. It's strangely common for people to hold on to reminders and mementos of negative experiences. (Note: If you've done that and have mementos that you've kept specifically to help you remember what happened, then hold onto them for now. We're going to do something with those mementos later!)

To be clear, when I tell you to wallow in your pain, I am *not* telling you to ruminate. "Feeling the bad" is different from ruminating, because you're not going over and over specific incidents. It's one thing to think through a scenario and probe at the thing that triggered your feelings. It's another to do it repetitively.

Instead of ruminating, which is cycling, you're going to take a straight path *through* the feelings and poke around as you go.

YOUR HOMEWORK:

Feel those feelings and wallow a little. Stay present with your pain. Journal about it. Start to probe around in the feelings and assess the source of your pain and your history.

[8]

Step One, Part Two: Expel the Pain

HOORAY! YOU'RE STILL ALIVE after the wallowing! Okay, now here's where I'll reveal a little bit of "big coaching magic:" I'm guessing that at some point during the last week, you started to feel better.

It's hard to feel bad when you're trying to *make* yourself feel bad. And you can only do it for so long. So by now, you probably feel much better. You may also feel better because you actually let yourself feel your feelings without pushing them away.

If you don't feel better yet, that's okay. That's what the next step in this process is all about.

Starting today, you're going to *officially* begin to let go of all that pain. You've already begun that process indirectly, but now you're going to get serious about it.

Not long ago, I had a client who went through the RE-BOUNDS Program. When she got to this part of the process and I told her what this step was all about, she exhaled loudly and said, "Oh, thank *God*." It was as if she had been carrying around an enormous burden, waiting for someone to relieve her of it for ages, and all she needed was *permission* to let it go.

Sometimes during a setback, we actually feel bad because we think we're supposed to feel bad. Sometimes we feel bad because we're angry at the world. Sometimes it's because things didn't meet our expectations. Sometimes it's because we're angry with ourselves for not doing the best that we could have done. I'll bet you have some of your own reasons why you felt bad. There are so many reasons to feel bad during a setback, right? And, wow, have you felt them lately!

But there are *also* reasons to feel good. It's often hard to see those reasons when you're in the midst of the setback. That's why it's awesome that you're no longer in the midst of your setback...right? Now that you're at the beginning of an upward swing, you'll start seeing all kinds of reasons to feel good.

STEP ONE, PART TWO: EXPEL THE PAIN

In fact, that's where you're going to start this week. You're going to start with a gratitude exercise. The research shows again and again that a daily gratitude practice leads to a generally more positive outlook on life.

One of my clients who started her gratitude practice found it so helpful that she began teaching her 5 year-old daughter to do it. That's how you change the world! The daughter shared the gratitude exercise with her friends, too. Imagine what a spectacular outlook these kids will have, if they continue to focus their attention on what they're grateful for as they grow into adulthood!

A gratitude practice will help you get started moving toward the future. But...what about all those bad feelings?

SIFTING THROUGH THE BAD FEELINGS

This week you're going to have to start sifting through those bad feelings you dealt with in the first part of Step One. You'll want to sort them into categories: the feelings that are about you, the ones that are about things that happened to you when you were growing up, the ones that are about feelings of injustice or unfair treatment, and the ones that are about other things. Let's dissect that for a minute.

Sifting through the feelings can be challenging, because our feelings are often like a big bowl of spaghetti. You can see that there are lots of different noodles in the bowl, but untangling them and figuring out which noodle is which can get tricky.

Sifting through the feelings can be challenging, because our feelings are often like a big bowl of spaghetti. You can see that there are lots of different noodles in the bowl, but untangling them and figuring out which noodle is which can get tricky.

This is one of those times when ideally, I would be right there with you, helping you untangle this mess. For now, I'll help you with some strategies for the untangling.

Meditation can be an excellent time for sifting through your feelings. Most people think meditation is all about sitting in the lotus position and humming some mantra to yourself, "Ohhhhm, Ohhhhhm," but it totally doesn't have to be like that!

For one of my podcasts, I interviewed Meghan Markle's meditation teacher, Light Watkins, author of the book, *Bliss More*, in which he clears up a lot of the myths about meditation, and makes it a whole lot easier[13].

If the idea of meditation makes you uncomfortable, then Light recommends that instead of "meditatiing," you just try sitting and thinking...or thinking in the shower. I do some of my best thinking when I'm letting my hair conditioner soak in. Plus, there are lots of apps that help with guided meditations as well.

You'll likely have experienced some feelings about yourself. Most people do. Search within and look around. Examine your feelings. You're looking for hallmarks of residual negative feelings about yourself, which are typically a feeling that you're not worthy, that you don't deserve success, that you aren't good enough, or that you've been fooling people and you just got caught (also known as "impostor syndrome"). These feelings will be the more challenging ones to rid yourself of, because they've likely been there a long time. Set these feelings aside for now. We'll come back to them shortly.

If your setback was an event that happened - a divorce, a breakup, a bad job performance review - then you'll probably have some feelings about that event. These feelings are often grief-related. You saw yourself with a particular future - married to your spouse, getting the next job, etc. - and now the future looks different from what you'd planned or at least, it's unclear what it will look like. The feelings that occur when you lose something that's important to you, like a job, a spouse, or a vision of the future, are typically grief.

Your setback might be an injustice. You didn't get the promotion because of unconscious (or overt) bias, or your significant other believed something about you that wasn't true and broke up with you, for example.

As you uncover the connection of feeling to cause, you may also discover some things that simply don't make sense. It's not uncommon to find misplaced anger, unfair attribution of responsibility, and more, as you go through this process. That's okay. You'll deal with those things in Step Two.

When You Can't Find the Source of the Feelings

There will invariably be some feelings for which you can't easily identify the source. When we can't figure out where a feeling comes from, one of the first places to look is your childhood.

Over the years, I've seen that clients from similar cultural backgrounds tend to share similar childhood wounds.

In a fantastic book called *Getting the Love You Want*[14], author Harville Hendrix talks about "childhood wounds." Everyone has these wounds. They come from damage caused by the people closest to us in our formative years. It's important to know that in most cases, the damage wasn't caused intentionally. In fact, it's my own theory that damage can be caused *culturally* as well.

Over the years, I've seen that clients from similar cultural backgrounds tend to share similar childhood wounds. Those clients who come from German backgrounds, for example, tend to be pretty strict with and hard on themselves. One client came from an Irish background and had trouble taking credit for his success, because he'd always been told he had "the luck of the Irish" in him. And I could write an entire book, just on the emotional wounds of clients who come from minority groups that historically (and in many cases, currently) have been mistreated, and how those wounds impact them as adults, in relationships and in the workplace.

Sometimes a client is able to trace the same wound back several generations. For example, I once had a client whose great grandmother had suddenly become a widow. The great grandmother had to feed her two children, and so she traveled all over the county collecting any debts owed to her deceased husband. As she traveled with her children, she would tell her daughter that she must always have her own money, because one never knew what might happen to one's husband. The daughter grew up and found a way to always ensure her own source of funds, a remarkable feat in her time. She raised her daughter (my client's mother) to do the same, but somehow, as this philosophy of independence was passed down, the message became garbled and distorted, much like that child's game, "Telephone." My client's mother became mistrustful of men and taught my client that "you can't rely on a man." As a result, my client struggled to develop strong, positive relationships with men who were her equal, instead selecting men she could emasculate and boss around, and finding herself in divorce court when her husband decided he'd had enough.

Each of us has wounds that are borne of our experiences in life. The wounds get activated or "triggered" when someone behaves in a way that, either consciously or subconsciously, reminds us of the person or the experience that first harmed us. As we become aware of these wounds and their role in our reactions, we can begin to utilize that awareness in the moment, *before* we react to new stimuli or circumstances in the same old ways.

> *The research indicates that it is when we do nice things for others that we begin to feel more positive feelings toward them.*

For now, sift through those feelings, and name them and categorize them. Sometimes your awareness is a big step on the path toward releasing them. Sometimes the habits of reacting are like deep grooves in a vinyl record, and they can be tricky to release.

Back to meditation for a moment...one of my favorite authors, Wayne Dyer, talked about sending love to the people we are angry with, as a mechanism toward healing and forgiveness[15]. It sounds counter-intuitive, doesn't it? But in fact, the research indicates that it is when we do nice things for others that we begin to feel more positive feelings toward them.

To that end, another type of meditation that you can use to begin healing your anger is a "loving kindness" meditation. I've found some meditation videos on YouTube that were lovely visualizations. Sometimes I like to envision a white or gold light or sparkles surrounding me, emanating from me, then sending that light to someone I'm angry with. I envision that person surrounded by the white light of good and love that came from me and imagine them feeling pure love surrounding them.

It can be hard to offer others that level of love and kindness, and doing so takes some practice. What's important here is a deep understanding that you cannot change others. *You can only change yourself.* Holding onto anger harms you, and no one else. You may think that it harms others, but it's really you who suffers. This understanding is at the very heart of REBOUNDS.

(And if you *really* need to feel that you're getting back at someone, the reality is that, as George Herbert said, "Living well is the best revenge.")

> *Your why is the reason you're going to all this trouble to rebound from your setback, and it's something that can carry you through the difficult moments of your bounceback.*

THINK ABOUT YOUR WHY

During this step, you want to also begin to think about your "why." Why are you interested in a bounceback? Why is it important to you? Why does a bounceback matter at all? Your why is the reason you're going to all this trouble to rebound from your setback, and it's something that can carry you through the difficult moments of your bounceback. Therefore, gain some clarity on your why now, so that you know what you're working so hard for!

FUTURE PACING

As you begin to release your negative feelings, you also want to look toward the future with optimism. How do we do that? Well, you're going to start with the presumption that you're learning the skills now that you need to achieve your goals in the future, which means that you *will* achieve your goals in the future. You *will* become the version of yourself that you need to become to get where you want to go. With that belief, you can envision your future, stepping into it as if you *already are* that version of yourself.

Sometimes I'll have a client take out two 8 1/2" x 11" pieces of paper and write "Now" on one and "Future" on the other. I'll have her (and for the sake of clarity, I'm using "her," but it could just as easily be "him") put the pieces of paper on the floor, about two to three feet apart, and stand on the "Now" paper. I'll work with her to ensure she's fully present in the moment, in the *now*. Then, I'll have her prepare to move into the future. When she's ready, I'll have her step on to the "Future" paper and close her eyes. I'll encourage her to be fully present in the future as that new version of herself, seeing what she'll see, hearing what she'll hear, feeling what she'll feel, and really getting into the future experience. Sometimes this exercise can even help you to gain a clearer perspective on what that version of yourself will look like. Once she's spent some time in the future, I'll have her step back to "Now" and ensure she's fully back in the present moment.

You can do this same exercise at home! As you do the exercise, create the future as a positive place, where you've achieved the life you want, where you've rebounded fully and are thriving in life. You can, if you want to, get more specific with your time frames, so that the more general "Future" becomes "Future in 2 Years" or "Future in 10 years," for example.

Earlier in this chapter, I said we'd come back to the entrenched feelings you have about yourself. We're going to start working on them now. Those feelings are going to take some time to change, and changing them on your own can be tricky, but I'll provide you with some strategies for handling the moments when you might get stuck.

MENTAL HYGIENE

One of the first things you're going to do to change those entrenched feelings is engage in a little "mental hygiene." That's right, we're going to clean your brain by changing what you feed it.

> **We're going to clean your brain by changing what you feed it.**

We're going to start with social media. You know that Instagram feed? Time to fill it with positivity. My Instagram feed is full of beautiful images of nature, of the most beautiful cities in the world, of hilarious jokes and memes, and of positive, uplifting messaging. Particularly on Instagram, I focus my attention on beauty and joy, rather than worrying about what my friends or peers are doing. I've made Instagram my own personal wonderland, where I can be uplifted any moment of the day, just by looking at it.

You're going to do something like this, whether it's clearing your Instagram out and making way for positive, good messaging, or adjusting your Facebook feed with a filter or app, so you stop seeing all the negative stuff. Focus on the good, the beautiful, the happy and joyful. Look for body positivity accounts and follow them. Look for good news and light.

I'm not telling you that making the world look a certain way makes it into being that way, but for awhile, we need to feed your brain some really good stuff.

I'm not telling you that making the world look a certain way makes it into being that way, but for awhile, we need to feed your brain some really good stuff. It's like when you want your body to get healthy, you start feeding it fruits and vegetables, right? Well, think of this as juicing for the brain.

Pairing your social media cleanse with your gratitude exercise and meditation is a very strong start. If meditation intimidates you, try an app designed to help with meditations. I personally love a semi-guided meditation, and there are some really wonderful ones on YouTube as well. Start slowly. Just try two minutes or five, and see how it goes. Your mind doesn't have to be blank, but as thoughts come into your mind, try to let them pass through, rather than getting focused on any one meditation.

This is a great start for your second week. This work really matters, because it prepares you well for what you'll do in the next step.

It's also a solid beginning for changing those feelings about yourself. We'll continue to work on those throughout this process, a little in each step of the program.

Another thing I'd like you to do before wrapping up this step is to monitor your thinking over the next couple of days. What are recurring thoughts that pop into your head, especially the ones about you? Write them down and keep track of them. We'll use them later.

YOUR HOMEWORK:

Start with your gratitude exercise. Then, sift through your feelings, meditate, and consider the ways in which you might engage in a little mental hygiene. Track your recurring thoughts for two days - write down the recurring thoughts that you have about yourself.

[9]

Step Two: Evaluate the Feedback

WELCOME TO STEP TWO, where we're going to do something you probably don't want to do *at all*. Hooray! Seriously, don't skip any of these steps, even if you don't want to do them, or you won't really bounce back! This program isn't about doing the parts you like, it's about doing all the steps and putting in the effort to get you back on top. **I promise it will be worth it!**

In Step One, we prepared your brain for this step by filling it with all the right ingredients and getting you in the right mindset. Now we're going to go back to the setback event and look at personal responsibility.

Personal Responsibility

"Ewww, yuck. That's hard." That's what most clients tell me when we start this part. Except they're wrong. Accepting responsibility isn't *that* hard. It's just that, often, we dislike being honest with ourselves and admitting that we've played a role in the road to our own setbacks.

That's not to say that we're *always* culpable for all of the things that happen to us - there are many things over which we have no control. But taking responsibility for the things that you did contribute to your own setbacks is important to your bounceback. This is where we begin to assess where we need to grow, evolve, and change to really bounce back like a rock star.

Often, we dislike being honest with ourselves and admitting that we've played a role in the road to our own setbacks.

This step is like the beginning location on your GPS. It's an honest look at where we are now. A GPS knows where you are right now, but I don't. And often, we're not entirely honest with ourselves about where we are right now.

Imagine that you have to tell a GPS where you're starting from. That means you have to be honest with yourself, because if you're at the office, but you tell the GPS that you're at home, you're going to get the wrong directions, aren't you? That's why it matters that you have an honest appraisal of where you are right now in life.

You need a clear starting location so that you can map out the most accurate directions to your destination.

REVIEW YOUR FEEDBACK

In Step Two, we're going to review the feedback you've gotten during your setback. This can be a sticky step, because in the first part of Step One, you probably spent some time in "poor me" territory, where you blamed others for the things that have happened to you. (That's okay, everyone does it!)

While it is true that there are times when things happen to us that aren't within our control, this step is focused on empowerment. You're going to take control over your life, own it, and be brave enough to look at the feedback you've received with complete honesty and integrity.

It is *critical* that you **look at this feedback and ask yourself where you could improve.** You *must* get out of the "everybody hates me" or the "it's not my fault" spaces and into a mindset where you understand that all people are flawed, even those who appear the most "normal." That includes you! Yes, you, too, are flawed, and you have room to grow. You must be at least somewhat open to at least some of the feedback you've received in order to change for the better.

Begin to review your feedback, take stock, and assess. What do you need to pay close attention to and what do you need to change? Are there positives that you need to play up? What feedback do you need to pay close attention to?

If you had a negative job performance review, then you're going to go over your notes from the review and assess what it all means. You're going to take stock of the good, the bad, and the ugly. What did they say? Do you remember? Did you take notes, or do you have a printed copy of your review? Read through it all and sift through all of the information. Are there pieces of feedback that you can act upon? Are there improvements you can make to your leadership style, your presentation, your work?

Remember, we're going to take these pieces of feedback into Step Three, where we'll begin creating our roadmap, and into Step Four, where we'll be taking action on the feedback, so you want to get very clear on what areas need work. If you're going through a divorce or breakup, it's worthwhile to reflect back on the things your ex said to you during the relationship - the things that really set him or her off.

It's important to note that I'm talking about regular, average relationships with regular, average problems. If you've been in abusive relationships and haven't gone through therapy, your perspective may be pretty skewed, with respect to the feedback you received. If that's the case, now might be a good time to put this book down and get thee to a qualified therapist who specializes in abuse.

Each person that you choose to be in a relationship with will be like a jigsaw puzzle piece, matching the pegs of your personality with the grooves of their damage.

Even if you've not been in an abusive relationship, if you're working the REBOUNDS Program after a relationship type of setback, like a divorce or breakup, be careful with this part. Remember childhood wounds from the last chapter? Each person that you choose to be in a relationship with will be like a jigsaw puzzle piece, matching the pegs of your personality with the grooves of their damage (this happens with jobs, too!).

We typically choose a partner because they remind us, good and bad, of the people who were closest to us during our formative years. So while we instantly feel a connection to them, eventually they'll also trigger our childhood wounds, in a way that few others can. The way you trigger one significant other will be different from the way you trigger another. One might be triggered by your cluttery ways, another might be triggered by your need to control the remote.

While it's always healthy to look for ways to become a better human (as well as being tidier and sharing the remote), making changes to satisfy an ex-partner's wishes may not always result in satisfying a future partner, as their needs and particular wounds may be different.

This is simply one area where you want to use your common sense to ascertain which requirements are peculiar (like if a partner has an aversion to yellow bath towels for some deep-seated reason) and which ones are generally part of good conduct (like good remote control stewardship).

I was brought up in a talkative family. If you didn't interrupt someone, then you probably wouldn't get to speak. Add in a healthy dose of ADHD and my tendency is to interrupt *a lot*. I've had to work hard to improve on that habit, so that as a coach, I can listen effectively to my clients and *not* interrupt them. As a result, I rarely interrupt my clients, unless there's a good reason. But because I'm relaxed when I'm with my husband, I often forget that I'm trying to improve this area and end up interrupting him, frankly, far too much, by any reasonable standards.

Generally speaking, interrupting a lot is pretty rude. I think we can all agree on that. It's something I work on constantly, not just because it happens to be a trigger for my hubby (that poor, patient, sweet man), but because becoming a person who doesn't interrupt others is a nice way to be with everyone.

Look at the feedback you've received and assess whether it's something that makes sense for you to address in the grand scheme of being a better human. If you've gotten the same feedback from several significant others or from several bosses, that's a good sign that it's a piece of feedback you'll want to take into Step Three.

When we receive any feedback, it's often under emotional circumstances, so step back and try to look at the feedback without the intensity of the emotion you were feeling when you received it. In the REBOUNDS program, we include many exercises and strategies to help you diffuse and reduce the deep emotion that you may experience when remembering traumatic or upsetting moments, including showing you how to work with memories, how to adjust perspective, and helping you to step back from the intensity of your feelings when it's necessary.

Your goal in this step is to assess the feedback, decide what merits keeping and acting upon, and what you can discard. Once you've separated wheat from chaff, then you can move on to the next step.

A WORD ON MEMENTOS:

Remember the mementos we talked about before? The letters, emails, written job review feedback, reports, etc., remember those? Well, this is the step where you're going to use them.

Now that you've been through Step One and you've felt all the bad feelings quite thoroughly, you can review these mementos with more detachment. Examine them for any useful feedback and take note of that feedback.

Then...get rid of them. And here's where I'm going to differ from a lot of the coaches out there today. I'm going to tell you *not* to make a big deal out of ridding yourself of these mementos. No mourning, no ceremonial burning, none of that is necessary, and it gives too much importance to a remnant of the past.

You've already done the emotional work around this stuff, so you can pretty much just discard it without much thought (though if it has sensitive or personal information, I do recommend shredding).

Okay, so...gather useful data from the mementos, and then toss them. You're done carrying the burden of these mementos. You can let them go.

Your Homework:

Take personal responsibility for where you are today. Evaluate all of the feedback and gain clarity regarding which feedback you must act upon and which can be discarded.

[10]

STEP THREE:
BUILD A PLAN

IN STEP TWO, YOU focused on assessing feedback and admitting that some of it has validity and deserves your attention. Step Three is about crafting a plan to act on it. In this step, you're going to create an actual plan to make real changes in your life. You're going to create a roadmap for your own evolution and growth, and then you're going to commit to making those changes.

Step Three is where you'll go back to the list you created in Step Two and for each of the pieces of feedback you received that you've deemed "action worthy," you'll come up with a goal for taking action on that feedback, as well as actions to help accomplish each goal - a few ways that you can act on the feedback to make improvements and show real growth.

In this chapter I'll be talking about how to make the changes you've decided to make to become the best version of yourself. We'll be using S.M.A.R.T. goals[16] as a basis for our planning. I'll show you how to create a realistic plan for change and ways to plan so that you're able to lock in the changes that you want to make.

S.M.A.R.T. Goals

Let's start with defining a S.M.A.R.T. goal. A S.M.A.R.T. goal is an outcome that's Specific, Measurable, Achievable, Results-focused, and Time-sensitive. Each of these aspects is important to setting outcomes that can actually happen.

Specific

A specific goal is one that is stated very clearly, and in precise detail. So, "I will exercise for 45 minutes a day, four days a week," is a more specific goal than "I will exercise more."

You also want to state a goal in the positive, so "I will exercise for 45 minutes a day, four days a week," rather than, "I won't sit on my butt getting more out of shape." We want to move toward the positive! (There *is* some evidence that delving briefly into what you *don't* want is also useful. You don't really want to stay here, but it's constructive to gain clarity about what you don't want and why you don't want it, but then move right into what you *do* want.)

Measurable

A measurable goal is one that you can measure (gasp!) Very few coaches make use of metrics, and I've always thought that it was a shame that they don't.

As Peter Drucker famously said, "What you can't measure, you can't improve." I've found that when a client can actually see that he or she has made progress toward a goal, and it's represented in the numbers, they're even more motivated to keep progressing. And motivation and accountability are two necessary ingredients for effecting long-term change and growth.

Let's look at an example to help you see how seeing your progress metrics can be effective. One of my clients, Mark, had gotten in over his head at work and, as a consequence of a busy work schedule, he was drinking too much coffee, eating too much fast food, and exercising way too little. He had neglected his health completely. He found himself out of breath when he took the stairs, and he was tired all the time.

> *"What you can't measure, you can't improve."*
> *- Peter Drucker*

Mark's setback was a health scare. One night he thought he was having a heart attack, but fortunately, it turned out to be a panic attack, brought on by too much stress and not enough self-care. Even before that night, he had been getting feedback in the form of heart palpitations, trembling, insomnia, and lack of focus. These were the messages that his body was sending to him. When he didn't listen, it started screaming, demanding that he listen.

Mark's health scare was enough to motivate him to take care of himself, but he needed help. The lure of fast food, caffeine, and sweets is very strong, and the feeling of laziness that comes with them can make it very hard to start exercising and stay on a healthy track, so support is critical to success when it comes to improving your diet and exercise.

Mark joined the REBOUNDS Program, and right away, he spent a week feeling sorry for himself and being annoyed with himself for letting things go so far (Step One, Part One), then released those feelings and created a picture of himself as a healthy, strong, and happy father for his children and a joyful, vibrant husband to his wife (Step One, Part Two). Then began to sift through the feedback his body had been giving him to determine what to do next (Step Two).

Once he had that clarity, we were able to develop a road-map for him to make changes...and that brings us back to metrics.

For our REBOUNDS clients who are working toward wellness goals, we set up a complete program where clients check in every day to report in about their exercise, eating habits, self-care, and more, to stay accountable and on-track. They're reminded via text or email to check in, which helps them remain mindful of the goals they're working towards throughout the day.

Each week, I personally review their metrics and send an encouraging note, some supportive suggestions, or just a delighted cheer. And when they check in with me on the phone for our sessions, we go over what's working and what isn't working and adjust the plan accordingly.

How do we know what's working and what isn't? Metrics and measurement! We set goals at the outset of the program, and then all of our clients' check-ins show us exactly where each client is making progress and where they're not. It sounds so simple, but it's amazing how many coaches don't use tools like this, and instead, just fly by the seat of their pants, relying on the client's sense of whether things are working.

When we don't have metrics, we don't have an accurate picture of what we're doing and how well it's working. Have you ever kept a food journal? Aren't you almost always surprised by how much you actually eat? It's the same with metrics - you'd be surprised by just how enlightening they are. Metrics allow you to see exactly how you're making progress. Measurement means you can see your progress as you get closer to your goals *and* you become more motivated in the process.

Measurement means you can see your progress as you get closer to your goals and you become more motivated in the process.

In fact, I recently tested out a new tracking system we're using to help clients stick to fitness goals. The initial version of the system lasted 30 days. I didn't think much of it, until around Day 35, when I realized that, after a month of consistent progress, I had really fallen off the wagon in the past week and couldn't figure out what had changed.

It wasn't until Day 38 that I realized that I had stopped receiving my reminders to check in, and therefore my attention had shifted away from my own fitness goals. With that shift, my health became less important, while everything else took priority. As soon as I restarted the tracking system, I immediately got back to consistent levels of activity. Once again, the value of measurement and metrics proved themselves to me! The system is now designed for six months, long enough to build a strong foundation for a new habit.

ACHIEVABLE

Let's talk about <u>achievable</u> goals, since that's the next part of building a S.M.A.R.T. goal. Achievable goals are realistic. But how do you determine what's realistic?

Have you ever planned a day full of activities or errands, and maybe you got to the end of that day and realized you'd *really* over-booked your day? Or maybe you have a to do list, and it never gets completed? Typically, the reason all of these things happen is because you haven't been realistic in your planning.

Remember that you do want to push yourself a little bit with these goals. Give yourself a bit of a stretch, a challenge. Aim a little higher than you think you can handle. Doing so helps you to see what you're made of.

Realistic or achievable planning involves thinking carefully about what is actually possible in a particular timeframe. Can you realistically drive anywhere in Los Angeles in five minutes? Not really. So it wouldn't make sense to plan as if you could. Can you realistically learn how to be an effective leader in a week? It's very unlikely.

Creating an achievable goal starts with thinking carefully about what's possible in the real world and taking into account the potential challenges and problems that might come up in the process.

So, for example, "I will lose 25 pounds in two weeks," probably won't be achievable (or sustainable), but at a normal, healthy rate of weight loss of about one to two pounds per week, with a little padding built in for family dinners/ holidays/ vacation/cheating/plateaus, "I will lose 25 pounds in 12-14 weeks," is much more realistic, achievable, and sustainable.

As for learning soft skills and leadership skillsets and building new habits, if you want your goal to be achievable and lock in the new habits, you'll be wise to give yourself at least a six-month timeline.

Remember that you do want to push yourself a little bit with these goals. Give yourself a bit of a stretch, a challenge. Aim a little higher than you think you can handle. Doing so helps you to see what you're made of. We rarely know what we're capable of until we push ourselves further than we think we can handle.

RESULTS-FOCUSED

A results-focused goal is one that focuses on the ultimate outcome of the goal, rather than the activities done to achieve that goal.

So the goal would be more like, "I will improve my confidence levels by 50% by July 12, 2019," rather than, "I will work with a coach who uses metrics so that I can measure and track my progress toward improving my confidence," the latter being a solid part of your plan, but not the actual goal.

TIME-SENSITIVE

Time sensitivity is important when you set a goal. If you don't have a little of the tension that urgency requires, then you're less likely to follow through on a goal. Urgency helps keep you motivated and moving forward.

Have you ever had a book sitting on your nightstand? I'll bet you have. I'll bet you've put that book on your nightstand, planning to read it. Did you? How many times have you planned to do something "soon" and realized that months had gone by without you doing it?

Adding some time-sensitivity to a goal helps you put a little pressure on, so that you're more likely to achieve the goal. Of course, you have to remember that the *why* is equally important. You can put a book on your nightstand and tell yourself you're going to read it within the next week, but if you don't have a good reason to do so, *and* there's something you'd rather do instead, then that book will probably still be sitting there, waiting to be read in a couple of months.

The Plan Behind the Goals

Once you've figured out what your goals are, now you can begin to plan what's behind the goals. How you plan to achieve the goal is dependent on the goal itself.

When you're talking about changing who you *are*, it's best to think either in full-out extremes or baby steps. That statement sounds pretty contradictory, so let me explain.

Full-Out Extremes

If you're going to make a change to a behavior, something that's easy to look at and say, "I am either doing this or I'm not," then that's probably a good thing to look at in terms of full-out extremes. Remember my interrupting example from the last chapter? I either interrupt or I don't. I don't have to *learn* how not to interrupt, I just have to become more mindful, remain present in my interactions, and practice good listening. Some habits are better handled "cold turkey."

Remember, habits are like grooves in a record. Sometimes those grooves feel like giant ditches, don't they? But there's really only one way out, and that's by deciding right here and now that you are *not* going to let yourself engage in that habit anymore, and you're going to change it *now*.

Also, remember that it can take from six months to even as long as a year to change a habit and form a new groove in that record. Your roadmap should be created for that duration - at least six months to a year - and you need to commit to being in this for the long haul. It will be worth it, I promise!

So the first thing you're going to do is sift through the feedback that you decided merited consideration. Is there anything in there that sounds like

> *In most cases, keeping a switch flipped is about remembering to keep it flipped.*

the kind of habit I've just described? If so, write that down. You have a switch that needs to be flipped, and we're going to flip it.

How can you make sure you flip the switch and keep it flipped, though? In most cases, keeping a switch flipped is about *remembering* to keep it flipped.

Think about it. You start your day with the best of intentions. You're probably doing great with keeping that switch flipped, until about mid-morning, when something distracts you. A problem, a hiccup, a challenge, or just something that catches your attention. And then it happens...you're quickly back to your old ways, and kicking yourself that afternoon or evening when you realize that you lost track of your goal.

But what if, instead, you had a system of reminders and accountability that help you to stay mindful? With my RE-BOUNDS Program clients, I use an online system that we call "The Trampoline," which allows us to set up all kinds of fantastic strategies to help our clients to stay mindful and remain on top of their goals.

This works with both the baby steps goals and the "switch flipping," full-out extreme goals. We're able to send out email and text reminders to our clients, plus we've set up strategies to help our clients stay accountable and track their progress with metrics. All of these tools helps you to keep your transformation goals at the top of your mind and to remain in progress.

Baby Steps

What if your goal isn't something that's a habit, but instead, it's a skill that you need to develop or a part of yourself that you want to improve? For example, what if you need to develop leadership skills or soft skills, or you want to become more confident?

These are the kinds of skills that fall into the "baby steps" category, because you can't really say, "I'm going to just be confident now," or "I'm going to be a good leader now." Certainly, you can "act as if" you are more confident, for example, and in many cases, this is a very useful exercise that can help you to experience a shift. But these shifts are largely temporary, and can't help cover the gap in an actual skillset that needs to grow.

These goals need to be planned out a little differently. You can still use a system like The Trampoline, but we tend to use it slightly differently for the "baby steps" outcomes.

With a baby step goal, you'll want to build in training (learning new information), coaching (working with someone who can help you integrate the new information), and rehearsal (practicing using the new skills), so it should be a gradual evolution, rather than a flipped switch.

These goals also require a period of time to "lock in" the new knowledge and habits, and they tend to take a little longer to build on the front end.

Once you have your plan in place, it's time to start acting on the plan.

YOUR HOMEWORK:

Set S.M.A.R.T. goals for each piece of feedback, then create action items to achieve each goal.

[11]

Step Four: Overhaul Yourself

YOU'VE REVELED IN THE bad and expelled it. You've evaluated all of the feedback you've received and separated the wheat from the chaff. You've built a plan to begin making changes. Congratulations! You've made it to the part where you actually begin implementing changes - you're ready to overhaul yourself!

In Step Four, things get serious! This step is where most people give up, because you've hit the moment where rubber meets the road. But not you! You're going to keep going and prove your mettle. Right? RIGHT!

Throughout this chapter, I'll give you some tips and strategies to help you through the "sticky" moments - the parts where you're most likely to get stuck - and to help keep you on track.

Making Things Real

Fact: It's *easy* to "feel the bad" and plan for the future. It's *harder* to enact that plan and make it real.

Up to this point, you've been doing emotional work, which can often *feel* less tangible and less real than the work you'll be doing from here on out.

Fact: It's easy to "feel the bad" and plan for the future. It's harder to enact that plan and make it real.

Oftentimes, the reason clients get stuck here is because it's easy to envision yourself as the you that you want to be, the best version of yourself, but because becoming that version of you takes a lot more work and effort, it's much more difficult to get motivated.

Plus, it can be a little scary to start putting these plans in motion. You might be nervous that you'll fail. You might be worried about what others will think. You might be worried about what you'll think. And you might be scared to put yourself out there to try again.

That's why the first "sticky" place in Step Four is starting this step at all. *That's why you need to understand your why.*

MOTIVATION: YOUR "WHY"

A while ago I told you that you needed to get clear on your "why." Your why is the reason that it's important to you to become the best version of yourself.

One of my clients, Evelyn, told me that her why was that she wanted to teach her daughters that women don't need to be limited in their accomplishments and achievements. She wanted to be an excellent role model for her children, and for them to see her succeed.

It's important that your why be something that motivates you when things get hard and when you get into an "I don't wanna" head space.

When Evelyn came into one of her sessions one day and said, "I'm so tired of working so hard to get promoted. When I think about getting to the next level, I just want to forget about it. It's too hard," I reminded her of what she'd said about her daughters, and asked if she'd changed her mind. Evelyn realized she'd let the day-to-day get in the way of her bigger aspirations, and her why is what pulled her out of a destructive mindset and back into positive action.

WORKING THE PLAN

In Step Three, you came up with your S.M.A.R.T. goals and actions that would lead you to each goal. Now is the time to work that plan.

Start by examining every action you wrote for your S.M.A.R.T. goals. Each action should be broken down into manageable pieces. In many cases, you'll need to break an action down into multiple pieces, so that you end up with a list of actions that can be done either daily (if they need to be repeated, like a good habit) or over a relatively short period of time.

If your actions are too big, you'll find them overwhelming and you'll get stuck. If your actions are too small, you'll get lost in minutiae and you'll get stuck.

At the same time, balance is key. If your actions are too big, you'll find them overwhelming and you'll get stuck. If your actions are too small, you'll get lost in minutiae and you'll get stuck.

MAKE YOUR ACTIONS MANAGEABLE

Jim came to me in the midst of a full-blown midlife crisis. He was in the process of getting a divorce, didn't like his career, and had let his health and fitness go. One of his S.M.A.R.T. goals was to make a major career decision within a specific timeframe. The action behind it was "Choose another career." You can imagine how an action that broad might trip Jim up. In fact, I'd argue that Jim had that action in mind before he even called me, and he was stuck there, because "Choose another career" is a *really* big action.

Jim and I worked together to break "Choose another career" into some manageable steps. Jim started by journaling about his current career and what he liked and didn't like about it, as well as taking some aptitude tests and job shadowing a few friends and acquaintances who were in jobs he thought he might enjoy. While certainly Jim did choose another career within his specified timeline, he did it by breaking that big, unwieldy action into much more manageable, less daunting tasks.

MAKE SURE YOU KNOW HOW

A few years ago, Mary came to me because she'd become overwhelmed by the politics in her office. There was so much jockeying for position and gossip, it was hard to keep it all straight.

The consistent feedback Mary got from her performance evaluations was that, while Mary was excellent at building relationships, she wasn't great at forging alliances that would work to her advantage (and theirs) and help her in this highly-charged political environment. Mary desperately needed allies who could help her to achieve her goals, and whom she could also help.

During Step Three, Mary created her S.M.A.R.T. goals and her actions to support the goals. When I reviewed her goals, I noticed that one of her actions was, "Build effective alliances." Hm....I asked Mary if she knew how to build effective alliances, and she said she wasn't sure she did.

Can you see where this action could easily get Mary stuck? If you create an action, but you don't know how to do that action, you'd better create a "learn how to" action that precedes it. You'll want an action like, "Learn how to [insert action here] by reading [insert book or article name here], by [insert date here]," for example.

Mary easily could have gotten stuck before she even started, and might never have built solid and effective alliances. Instead, she was able to learn the necessary skills to build those alliances before she began trying to build them, which made her much more effective in choosing the right allies and more strategic as she got to know them.

If you don't know how to accomplish a step, then *learning* how to accomplish that step is probably a good preceding step.

METRICS

You know by now that I'm a firm believer in metrics. Many coaches don't make use of them, and I don't know if it's because they're challenging or because they don't have the right tools, but I think it's a big mistake not to use them. I believe in metrics so much that I'm including two sections about them in this book!

As you watch metrics improve *and* see the results of those improvements, whether you're seeing your skill level go up, your weight go down, or even something like your feelings of confidence rise, you'll naturally be more motivated to continue making progress.

But because it's not the measurement that motivates you, you must be careful in selecting what to measure. It's not just pounds or inches lost in a weight loss journey, for example, but overall daily energy ratings, sick days (which should go down the more you take care of yourself, mind and body), and recording those "NSV" (non-scale victories) that helps you see your progress.

I've had clients who chose not to keep track of metrics in this process, so I built in my own semi-secret metrics to track *something* for myself, so I could see the trends. They had no idea how they were doing, and their present state of mind dictated how they rated themselves overall.

When I inquired about their overall confidence levels on days when they were feeling confident, they tended to rate their overall confidence as high. But when they were having less confident days, they rated their overall confidence as significantly lower.

Their current state had so much influence over their perceptions that it was impossible to gain a clear picture of whether their confidence was improving in the aggregate. As soon as they agreed to take a more systematic approach, they became much more attuned to their true progression.

In addition, as you observe metrics, you can assess what's working and what isn't. When you're working on a weight loss goal and you keep a food and activity journal, you can look back at what you ate and did the week prior, and usually see why your weight went up. When you're working on building your self-confidence, a journal will help you assess what happened the day of and the days before a low rating, so that you can start to think about ways to increase your resilience to whatever happened that lowered your confidence.

Metrics help you see your progress and tweak your strategies for maximum impact. Without them, you're flying blind, and your journey will take much, much longer.

Metrics help you see your progress and tweak your strategies for maximum impact. Without them, you're flying blind, and your journey will take much, much longer.

These are the reasons why metrics are such an important part of the REBOUNDS system. Our online tools are designed to help REBOUNDS clients see just how well they're doing and make changes when they're needed.

Go!

Here's the thing: I can write a lot more. I'm pretty verbose. But it's time for you to start *doing*. Don't worry: I'll be here when you get back!

In fact, what I'd like for you to do right now, before you get to the homework or anything else, just **do one thing today that gets you closer to one of your goals.** Just one thing. Once you've done that thing, you can read the rest of this chapter. *GO!*

Did you do it? Did you do your one thing? If you didn't, go back and do it now. It's just one thing.

REALITY CHECK

Here's the brutal, honest truth: No one will solve your problems for you. No coach can fix you. No therapist can repair you. No doctor can heal you. The reason is that eventually, all fixing, repairing, and healing requires something from *you*.

> *It's time to be your own hero and take whatever action you need to take to become the best version of yourself.*

If you want to see real change in your life, it's going to take honest effort from you to make that change happen. No one is going to do it for you. It's time to be your own hero and take whatever action you need to take to become the best version of yourself.

This step is the step I can't do for you. I can give you all the tools and strategies, and I can lead you through this bounce back. But I can't *make* you do anything. Only you have the power to do that. And make no mistake about it, you *do* have the power.

As you'll learn in the next chapter, it won't always be easy. There'll be barriers and obstacles in the road ahead. But you can conquer just about anything when you do as my dad used to tell me, and "keep your eyes on the prize."

You'll be tested in this step more than in any other. Everything up to this point has been easy in comparison. Brace yourself and know that you *are* up to the challenge.

As my friend Diamond Dallas Page (DDP) says, "Whether you say you can or you say you can't, you're right." Be strong, be brave, and be your own best ally in your fight to become the best version of yourself.

YOUR HOMEWORK:

Review your S.M.A.R.T. goal actions and revise them according to the guidelines in this chapter. Set metrics to match your actions and track your progress as you begin to implement your plan.

[12]

STEP FIVE: UNDERSTAND RESISTANCE

RESISTANCE IS A FORM of roadblock or challenge that keeps you from accomplishing your goals. Now that you're actively working your plan, you'll most likely begin to encounter resistance in two forms: internal and external.

It's important for you to learn how to see these forms of resistance for what they are and have some strategies in your back pocket to manage them when they crop up. That's what we'll be focusing on in this chapter.

INTERNAL RESISTANCE

Internal resistance stems from something I call "brain junk." In my first book, *Business in Blue Jeans*, I defined brain junk as "the mental baggage that gets in your way, and it can stop you...*before you've even started.*" It's basically all the negative self-talk, the voices in your head that typically say things like, "I can't because...," "I shouldn't because...," "I'm not good enough/smart enough/I don't have enough money to....," "I'm not worthy to...," and any other beliefs and ideas that prevent you from taking action and/or accomplishing your goals.

Your brain junk can quickly form internal resistance in a variety of ways. For example, it can trick you into believing you're not worthy of achieving your goals. I call this "Grasshopper Mode," based on a story I read many years ago in the Bible about the children of Israel who, upon reaching the Promised Land, were afraid to enter, because there were already people living there. The verse says, "And there we saw the giants and we were in our own sight as grasshoppers, and so we were in their sight" (Num. 13:33 KJV). They were afraid they didn't measure up to the people who were living in *their* Promised Land, even after *God* told them they were his chosen people.

> *It's important to remember that we all have moments when we experience grasshopper mode, even the most successful among us. Successful people experience fear and self-doubt and brain junk, too. We just know how to handle it when it crops up.*

Grasshopper Mode happens to everyone. Maybe you see people in leadership in your company, people who are further along in their careers, or people who are at the top of your field and you think, "Wow, those people are amazing. I'll bet they never experience self-doubt or insecurity."

Would it surprise you to know that *most* CEOs experience impostor syndrome (that feeling that you're going to be "found out" at any time, and "they" will realize you've been faking it the whole time)? They're *really* good at hiding it, but it's there.

I've been working with people at the highest executive levels for almost 20 years, and I can tell you for a fact that *all* of them struggle from time to time.

What's fascinating is that when you see yourself as a "grasshopper" on a regular basis, you teach others that that is how you see yourself, and how they should see you as well. Each of us puts off a "vibe" that tells people how we see ourselves, and if you're putting off a "grasshopper" vibe, then you're telling others to see you as small and insignificant. But if you see yourself as someone who's on the verge of massive success, then that's how the world will see you, too.

It's important to remember that we all have moments when we experience grasshopper mode, even the most successful among us. Successful people experience fear and self-doubt and brain junk, too. We just know how to handle it when it crops up.

That's why I'm going to give you some of my favorite strategies, the things that will help you to conquer your brain junk.

YOUR HOMEWORK:

For every S.M.A.R.T. goal, close your eyes and meditate on the goal. Get inside the goal and inhabit it in your mind. Feel what it feels like to have already achieved each one of your goals. Hold onto that feeling.

THE VOICES IN YOUR HEAD

As you go about your day, there are different versions of you that are experiencing your day in different ways. There's a version of you that's in the moment, doing things. There's also a version of you that's observing you doing things, and there's a version of you that's judging and assessing and making a running commentary about you, your performance, the results you're getting, and everyone and everything around you.

In addition, you have voices in your head that are essentially the echoes of all kinds of people that you've encountered in life, from family members and friends to bosses and coworkers to teachers and professors. They're all in there, they all have something to say, and in general, we tend to make the mistake of listening to their messages and believing them.

Over the years I've had clients who told me all kinds of things that they believe about themselves. One client had been told that no one who owns a business can be successful. Another client was told that any measure of success that he achieved was because he was lucky. Another client said she was sure that if she didn't get another client, she'd end up down in a van by the river.

All of these things were things that people had said to my clients at one time or another (or repeatedly over time), and for whatever reason, their brains latched onto the messaging and held onto it for good.

For many years, I believed a voice in my head telling me that any big success I had would hurt other people. I even thought that the voice was mine. During one of my own bouncebacks, I questioned that voice, and I discovered where the messaging actually came from and realized that *I* didn't believe that messaging at all. I knew it wasn't true.

Sometimes the realization alone that the voice in your head is telling you things that aren't true, that aren't even your ideas, is powerful enough to transform you. Sometimes it helps just to name it, so when it crops up, you can fight it.

> *Sometimes the realization alone that the voice in your head is telling you things that aren't true, that aren't even your ideas, is powerful enough to transform you.*

Sometimes you have to do a little internal negotiation. Maybe a voice in your head has been telling you that if you listen to some of the feedback from your ex-spouse, then you have to listen to all of it. It's constructive to explore whether there's a part of you *now* that recognizes that listening to everything someone says about you isn't necessary, but it can be useful to assess which parts of their feedback may be worthwhile. You can certainly have a little sit-down with yourselves and let them hash it out. Sometimes I even encourage clients to let disagreeing parts of themselves negotiate with one another to settle on an agreement they can both live with. In the REBOUNDS program, I teach clients exactly how to do these negotiations so that they're successful.

This is another time when journaling is really helpful. If you take just two days and log all of the negative thoughts you have in those two days, you'll get closer to mapping out your brain junk, so that you can begin to see patterns and address them.

Your Homework:

One of my most favorite homework assignments to give clients is the Inventory of Success. The Inventory of Success is a document in which you curate your lifetime of achievements. It's a living document of all the fantastic things you've done in your life.

Include anything you can think of, going back as far into your childhood as you want. Keep this document updated as you log more and more achievements, and bring it out to remind yourself of how awesome you are when you are feeling low.

This chapter is unusual, in that I've already given you two homework assignments and we're not even halfway through! But these assignments will help you, so please don't skip them!

THE BIG STRETCH

One of most important things when you're working your plan is to be prepared for The Big Stretch. When you do things that make you uncomfortable, you're stretching your boundaries. *And that is a very good thing.*

Most mornings, I do a little yoga. I like the strength and flexibility it gives me. You know that pull in your muscles that you feel when you stretch? That's one of my favorite feelings! Did you know you can get that kind of stretch in your brain, too?

Your brain works the same way as your muscles, when you're pushing yourself and stretching your boundaries. Some days will be easier. Other days, based on your mindset that day, will be harder. But the more you stretch, the more things will get comfortable for you.

When you do things that make you uncomfortable, you're stretching your boundaries. And that is a very good thing.

If you're scared to talk to people in leadership at your company, for example, then try to talk to the people in leadership who seem the friendliest, and gradually work your way to the most intimidating. This gradual approach is one way of stretching the boundaries of your comfort level and continuing to grow.

Successful people are always pushing their boundaries, so that they can continue to be comfortable with being uncomfortable, which keeps them in a constant state of growth.

EXTERNAL RESISTANCE

For some, it's the external resistance that creates a dilemma. External resistance is the resistance that comes from other people and circumstances.

NAYSAYERS, NEGATIVE NELLIES, AND TOXIC PEOPLE

Have you ever had a naysayer in your life? Maybe you had a well-meaning friend who didn't want to see you get hurt? Or maybe you have someone in your life who actually doesn't mind if you get hurt. That person's probably likely to fall into the "toxic people" category. Then there are the "Negative Nellies," folks who spend an inordinate time focused on doom and gloom. If you have a lot of people of these types in your life, then you might be surrounded by people who are holding you back.

Whether the people in your life are trying to hurt you or help you, discouraging words can have a strong impact on your motivation. When you hear that people around you don't believe in you, it can seep into your consciousness and you can start to believe what they seem to believe, which can be a big problem, because *your belief in yourself is very important to your success.*

Your friends and the people you surround yourself with have a massive influence on your success.

It's also important to note that your friends and the people you surround yourself with have a *massive* influence on your success. Many people have heard and shared the quote by Jim Rohn, "You are the average of the five people you spend the most time with," but the research shows that in reality, you're far more influenced by your friends than you may realize.

The research shows that if your friend gains weight, you're 45% more likely to gain weight. If your friend smokes, you're 65% more likely to smoke. Happy friends make you happier. And negative friends make you more negative. Successful friends make you more successful. The influence of your social network is massive.

Limiting Exposure

Wherever possible, you should try to protect yourself, your belief in yourself, and your general mental well-being. It's generally best to limit your exposure to people who say negative things about your success or who are negative in general, including anyone who is "looking out for your best interests" by encouraging you to play small. It also includes the toxic and/or abusive people who tell you that you're not worthy of success.

> *Wherever possible, you should try to protect yourself, your belief in yourself, and your general mental well-being.*

This isn't just about naysayers and toxic people. This is also about the Negative Nellies who can bring you down.

One of my clients, Joe, worked with a team that went up for promotions at the same time. Some of them received the promotions, while others didn't. In the aftermath, Joe was reeling from the negative evaluation and the fact that he didn't get his promotion. He was devastated and hated that he had to tell his significant other that he didn't get the promotion and the raise that came with it.

When Joe hired me to help him through this setback, he mentioned the negative vibe at work. As he relayed how his coworkers who weren't promoted were talking with each other and about their bosses and their peers who were promoted, it began to dawn on Joe that spending time with these peers was bringing his mood down even more.

Joe realized that all the critical talk, gossip, and complaining was contributing to his feelings that none of the feedback he'd received was worth listening to.

A similar effect happens when people get divorced. The ex-spouses sit with their friends and denigrate their former partners. It's not that this isn't perfectly normal, because it *is*. However, doing so means that you stay in a negative, angry place, and *out* of an empowered place of recognizing that most divorces are the result of a failure on the part of *both* spouses, not just one. This is a mindset that keeps you destined for failure again and again and again.

Joe began to limit the time he spent with his Negative Nellie coworkers, and was able to focus his attention on making improvements in the areas his supervisor had mentioned in his review. As a result, when the next round of reviews came around, Joe was much better prepared, and this time, he was one of people who got the promotion. For the record, all of the others who hadn't gotten that first promotion had either left their jobs or failed to get the promotion a second time, and left shortly after that.

When You Can't Limit Exposure: Good Mental Hygiene

You can't always avoid people, however. You may have to work with or live with someone who's negative or toxic. So let's talk about how you can cope when you have to be around someone who's not great for your positive mental state.

Remember that gratitude exercise you started in Step One? Well, that exercise is a big piece of "good mental hygiene," which is really just taking care of your brain and your positive mental state. The research shows that a regular gratitude practice can help you maintain a positive mental attitude over time.

You won't be able to change others directly, though remember that research I was just talking about? You *will* have an influence on them, and they *will* have an impact on you.

If you must work with or spend time with a Negative Nellie, you'll have to actively try to minimize his or her effect on you.

While Joe was able to limit his exposure to the Negative Nellies at work, there were times when he had to work with them. On those days, he would spend extra time doing his gratitude exercises (sometimes doing them multiple times throughout the day) and meditating on loving kindness. Sometimes he would prepare himself the day before by sending himself beautiful and funny images that he could look at and enjoy whenever he felt their influence creeping in.

If you have negative or toxic people in your life, it's important that you compensate by adding more positivity into your brain. Combat the negative influence as much as you can, and keep things positive!

YOUR HOMEWORK:

Take a look around at your friends and the people you spend the most time with. Are they toxic, negative, or gen-

erally unsupportive of your growth? Consider how best to cope with the challenges of having these people in your life.

[13]

STEP SIX: NOTIFY IMPORTANT PEOPLE

OFTENTIMES, WE EMBARK UPON self-discovery and personal development projects privately. We prefer to keep our personal growth on the "down low." Why is that?

In general, culturally many people experience a certain amount of shame in admitting that they need help. They prefer to keep things quiet and not tell anyone they're working to improve themselves.

I've always thought that self-improvement is a thing worth celebrating, personally. It's a wonderful thing that you're doing, and when you're also working to improve yourself professionally, how can anyone fault you for that?

Many successful people understand that what got you to where you are today may not be the same things that get you to the next level. The executives I've worked with over the years have tended toward celebrating working with a coach and developing themselves.

In fact, that's why I added this step. I want you to understand the benefits of sharing with important people that you're doing this work.

I know you may feel reluctant or nervous about sharing this work with anyone. I understand. This is deeply personal work. You don't have to get into the particulars of specifically what you're working on. Just letting the important people know that you're doing this work can be beneficial.

> *You don't have to get into the particulars of specifically what you're working on. Just letting the important people know that you're doing this work can be beneficial.*

In addition, when you tell the people in your life that you're working on responding to some feedback that you've received, and letting them know that you could use some encouragement and support, you give them an opportunity to help you. We could all use more help, especially when we're working to improve ourselves.

When you tell people who are directly impacted by the work you're doing, like your boss or your spouse, you're telling them that you're stepping up in a big way. Taking action means a lot!

Another benefit of telling the important people in your life about what you're up to is that they'll be able to hold you accountable, too.

WHO ARE THE IMPORTANT PEOPLE?

It's not that you have to tell *everyone*, but there are some people who might be good people to tell that you're going through the REBOUNDS program, in particular, because it will help them to see you as someone who's interested in improving and making a real difference in your life. Ultimately, though, you get to decide who to tell and who not to tell.

YOUR BOSS

If you're doing the REBOUNDS program because you had a negative job performance review or appraisal, then it may be a good idea to tell your boss that you're doing this work in response to the feedback you received. It shows you've listened and are responding. I've been known to assign this conversation to my clients.

Taking the initiative to embark upon a program like REBOUNDS shows that you're serious about your career, heard the feedback in your evaluation session, and are different from most of the people who receive negative performance appraisals.

Taking the initiative to embark upon a program like REBOUNDS shows that you're serious about your career, heard the feedback in your evaluation session, and are different from most of the people who receive negative performance appraisals. It shows your boss that you're serious about your job and about your career, and you're not here to play around.

The way in which you tell your boss is important. Rather than just dropping it into a conversation, you may want to schedule a meeting to inform them of your progress since your evaluation.

Such a positive reaction to a negative performance review is so unusual that if you tell your boss that you're doing this, you will undoubtedly stand out as a rock star.

When you meet, let them know that you heard the feedback and that you've decided to pursue this program (even better if you can tell them that you're receiving individual coaching, which means hiring a coach, obviously). Ask them if there's anything in particular that they think you should work on with your coach, and let them know that you're looking forward to being better prepared for the next evaluation (you'll want to share this information with your coach as well).

Such a positive reaction to a negative performance review is so unusual that if you tell your boss that you're doing this, you will undoubtedly stand out as a rock star. Just taking the action of reading this book is far more than most people would do (and if you're this far into the book, congratulations, you're among the elite!)

One of my clients, Michelle, told her boss that she was working with me, doing the REBOUNDS program, after she didn't get a promotion that she'd been expecting. He was extremely impressed with her initiative, and began encouraging her and creating opportunities for her to demonstrate her capabilities to the leaders who made the decision about promotions. Guess who got the promotion next time around!

Your Co-workers

Remember when I said that your friends and co-workers influence you? Well, you influence them, too! So why not share REBOUNDS with them, especially if they're going through a similar challenge? If you see a co-worker struggling, share what's working for you. It just might help save their job.

Michelle, the client I mentioned earlier, shared RE-BOUNDS, along with some of her early results, with her co-workers. Some of them were too far down the road of negativity that happens all too frequently after job performance reviews go south. But a couple of them joined the program as well, and not only did it help improve overall morale, working the program alongside one another pulled their team together in a very positive way.

Your Spouse/Significant Other (or ex-Spouse/ Significant Other)

Maybe your marriage ended and you wish it hadn't. Maybe it's in trouble and heading toward divorce, and it happened (or is happening) in large part because of you (by this point in the program, you shouldn't be rejecting that notion). If this is the case, then it's worth considering telling your ex-spouse (or almost ex-spouse, if your divorce has yet to be finalized) that you're going through a program that encourages you to listen to the feedback you've been given and act upon it.

I can't promise you that you'll get your partner back. But I can tell you that many marriages have been saved by one partner critically assessing his or her role in the problems of the marriage and diving back in and giving it their all to fix every contribution they've made to the demise of the relationship.

Don't be surprised if you hear, "I'll believe it when I see it!" or something similar from your spouse. You'll have to show *real* growth for your partner to believe in you again. But if it saves your marriage, it's worth the effort, believe me. Remember, it'll be those daily reminders and metrics that will help keep you on track and making progress toward consistent improvement.

Your Doctor

If you've decided to use the REBOUNDS program for a health goal like weight loss or getting in shape, then I encourage you to check with your doctor first, just as you would for any diet or fitness program. Your doctor can probably also make some useful suggestions for ways to supplement the program.

Your Friends and Family

It's great to have a support network of people who can encourage and help you when you get stuck. If your friends and family are supportive, then it's great to get them on your team.

If they're not super-supportive and tend toward the Negative Nellie or naysayer (or worst case, toxic) side of things, then you may not want to bring them in for their kind of "help." That kind of help could end up being more destructive than beneficial.

Choose what you say and to whom you say it wisely. Be concise and let people know how they can help and support you.

Don't be afraid to leverage online networks for support as well. We maintain a private Facebook group for clients to support and encourage each other, since they're all going through the same program with the same steps. Coaches are there to help clients as well. We also have a Facebook page where folks who are reading the book and doing a DIY version of REBOUNDS can support each other (you can find it at fb.me/bouncebackartist)

A Word About Timing

Generally speaking, make sure you consider timing when you decide to share REBOUNDS with people. You may not want to just blurt it out or tell someone in passing, when there's no time to explain.

Pick a good time when there's plenty of time for you to explain the basics of REBOUNDS and why you've decided to pursue it, as well as what you hope the results will be after you've completed this work. Leave enough time for you answer any questions that the person might have.

YOUR HOMEWORK:

Make a list of the people you want to tell about the work you're doing. What do you think will happen if you tell them? This is a time to be brutally honest with yourself.

Practice telling them in the mirror. Stick to the basics.

And then (deep breath) tell them.

[14]

Step Seven: Deny Resistance

DIDN'T WE ALREADY COVER resistance? We sure did! But we're covering it again, because it is *so important* and will certainly impact you more than once, as you work your way through this program. Resistance will come up again and again as you work the REBOUNDS program, and it will come up in a variety of ways.

What are some other ways in which resistance may come up along the way in this program?

Are You Being Fully Honest?

One form of resistance that I'm always concerned about is that you may not have been fully honest with yourself. One of the challenges of being a coach is that you only get to see what the individual sees. I can only see the picture that you paint for me. If you're not being honest with yourself, if you're resisting facing truth about yourself and how others see you, then the help I offer can only go so far.

Part of my job is to encourage you to go as deep as you can and not just scratch the surface. And this is the *really* hard part: what stories are you telling yourself? What lies do you choose to believe in because the truth is too painful?

Sometimes we don't see ourselves clearly because we don't *want* to. After all, it's much easier to avoid seeing the truth about ourselves, right?

Sometimes we don't see ourselves clearly because we don't want to. After all, it's much easier to avoid seeing the truth about ourselves, right?

My client, June, saw herself as a pleasant, affable person people liked to be around. She believed she was an excellent leader to her team, and couldn't understand why they didn't seem to respect her or follow her lead. However, when she began to relay some comments she made to her employees, many of which were passive aggressive, negative comments or judgmental jokes, I began to realize that June wasn't being entirely honest with herself. She would complain about others' judgmental behaviors and comments, but wasn't able to see her own.

It's never easy to look honestly at ourselves and see our deepest flaws, but only when we do, can we change ourselves for the better. June had to come to terms with the ways in which her behaviors weren't matching up with her vision of the best version of herself, and take responsibility for changing those behaviors, so that she could become the person she wanted to be and saw herself as.

There are many ways in which we lie to ourselves, and it can cause all kinds of resistance to change.

DUAL LIVES

It's not uncommon for people to lead dual lives when they're lying to themselves. I'm not talking about the kind of life where you have completely separate families in different cities. I'm talking about holding two different beliefs simultaneously.

When you hold competing beliefs at the same time or when you think one way, but act another, you may experience cognitive dissonance, where you feel tense and psychologically uncomfortable.

Sometimes people justify their contradictory behavior with context: "I am stealing office supplies because they didn't give me the raise that I deserved." They feel justified in their actions and therefore do not perceive them as violating their beliefs about themselves as an honest person.

Sometimes people just find it easier to live a lie. James came to me after a financial set-

Sometimes people just find it easier to live a lie.

back in his business. He'd grown up wealthy and was used to buying whatever he wanted. When his business suffered a catastrophic setback during the Great Recession, James continued his financial life, as if nothing had happened. He couldn't bear to change his lifestyle, and didn't want to believe that he had to do so.

James was living dual lives. In one life, he spent whatever he wanted, buying clothes, going on trips and out to dinner with friends, ultimately racking up credit card debt like crazy. In the other life, he was struggling to keep his financial head above water, and paralyzed with fear about losing his house.

James' first step in REBOUNDS was getting honest with himself and choosing which life he was going to live. He chose to face his responsibility and stop accumulating debt. Part of his REBOUNDS meant telling his friends that he couldn't go out with them so frequently anymore. No more lavish dinners and travel for James. But he did it in an eloquent way that helped him preserve the dignity he felt he needed. Instead of saying, "Hey, friends, I'm broke," he told his friends he was working on achieving some financial goals (which was true) and wanted to pull back on any unnecessary expenditures while he did so. He paid off his debt and got his business back on track.

By the time he did those things, he had also gotten his head around the fact that he hadn't really needed to buy so many things anyway. He was buying stuff and spending money to prove that he was "somebody." In *not* doing those things while he paid off his debt, he realized he had been somebody all along, and he also realized who his real friends were. They were the ones who stuck by him the whole time.

The biggest element of resistance will be you. As long as you blame other people for your problems, as long as you farm out responsibility for change, as long as you wait for someone else to rescue you, you'll stay right where you are, in Setback Land.

The second you own your mistakes, weaknesses, and failures and acknowledge that there is useful information to be found in the feedback you receive, whether that feedback comes formally through a job appraisal, informally through comments from a spouse, or from an unexpected source like your bank account or your body, you will begin to see your life change. You'll begin your bounce back. But you absolutely *must* be fully honest with yourself to get there.

Remember that when you notify important people about your REBOUNDS journey, you may experience some pushback. Some people won't want you to succeed. Some people will want you to stay the way you are. Some people won't believe in you. And it's okay that they feel that way. You do not have to adopt their viewpoint!

> *The second you own your mistakes, weaknesses, and failures and acknowledge that there is useful information to be found in the feedback you receive, you will begin to see your life change.*

FIND SUPPORT STRUCTURES

If you struggle to find the support you need, if you find that you're encountering resistance at every turn, then you may need to hire a coach to help keep you on-track. When you're a REBOUNDS member, you get access not only to me and my coaching team, but also to other REBOUNDS members online who can help you stay focused on your goals, with your eye on the prize.

YOUR HOMEWORK:

Dig deep and ask yourself tough questions. Are you being fully honest with yourself? Are you living with incompatible beliefs? Find the support structures that will help you grow, encouraging you along the way.

[15]

Step Eight: SOAR!

WELL, HERE WE ARE. You've been through seven steps, you've felt the pain and released it, you've honestly assessed the feedback you've received and where you are today. You've made a plan, dealt with resistance in many forms, and you've started to implement your plan. Now it's time to soar.

It might sound scary to you. "What, soar? Me? Now?" But it's time. You've laid the groundwork. You have a clear path ahead. You know what to do when things get challenging. And by now, you should have a supportive community surrounding you.

You've assembled all the tools for success. Now all you have to do is use them.

Prepare to Launch

Now that you've been through the other seven steps, you'll want to prepare your launch sequence. Your launch sequence includes steps actually based on NASA launches[17]:

- Setting up backup plans.
- Reviewing your plans.
- Testing systems.

- Clearing your launch pad.
- Purging any residual negativity.
- Loading fuel tanks.
- Checking the weather.
- Aligning antennas.
- Activating flight recorders.
- Locating and turning on internal power.
- Liftoff.

Yes, they really are based on NASA's launch sequence! Let's go through each of your steps:

SETTING UP BACKUP PLANS.

You'll begin preparing for liftoff by setting up any backup plans that are necessary for your launch. What if your first plan doesn't work? What's your failsafe?

REVIEWING YOUR PLANS.

Review all of your plans and look for holes. Have you missed anything? Are there any areas where you're likely to experience technical difficulties or hangups?

TESTING SYSTEMS.

Test your new strategies and systems to make sure they're working. How are things going? Is your gratitude practice working? This is where you'll find those metrics we talked about to be the most helpful.

CLEARING YOUR LAUNCH PAD.

Now is a great time to clean house. When you're ready for your relaunch, you don't want anything standing in your way. Do you have people in your life who are creating roadblocks, those Negative Nellies, naysayers, and toxic people we talked about before? Do you need to declutter your office? Do you need to purge your wardrobe? Clean out the pantry and refrigerator? Make sure you're clearing the way ahead by ridding yourself of anything that might get in the way of achieving your goals.

PURGING ANY RESIDUAL NEGATIVITY.

This far into the program, you should be seeing an improvement in your attitude, your setback, and the people in your life. If you're not, it's time to get serious about your mental hygiene. Where is the negativity coming from? What's the source? Start to dig into that source and root out the problem, so that negativity doesn't sap you of your positive energy and keep you from opportunity!

LOADING FUEL TANKS.

You're going to need energy. That means getting more sleep, eating healthier, and exercising. *I know, I know.* Nobody wants to hear that. It's no fun, but it's important.

You might be amazed to hear that the food you eat and how much you do or don't exercise has a *huge* impact on your mental health.

I used to suffer from pretty significant anxiety. My stomach was tied up in knots *all* the time, often for no reason at

all. When I changed my eating habits (cutting back on re-
fined carbs and processed foods, adding more fruits and
vegetables, and lean meats,
mostly), my anxiety miracu-
lously went away. I've tested

**You might be
amazed to hear that
the food you eat and
how much you do or
don't exercise has
a huge impact on
your mental health.**

it several times, trying a Mc-
Donald's lunch when I was in
a hurry (yes, I admit it), or eating some chocolate cake at a
birthday party, and the results
are the same every single time:
without fail, when I put junk in
my body, I experience anxiety.

I've also discovered that exercise helps a ton with anxiety,
depression, and ADHD. Two of my favorite books, *Spark* and
Go Wild, both by Dr. John Ratey, talk about the impact of exercise and nutrition on mental health (and even test scores,
which is why I've been eating healthy and exercising while
I've been writing this book! I wanted to give you my very
best!)

Plus, when you exercise and eat right, you have a better
shot at sleeping better. I call exercise, nutrition, and sleep
the Holy Triumvirate of Energy. You really need all three to
thrive.

CHECKING THE WEATHER.

You're going to have to look outside and see what the
weather looks like, once you've cleared your launch pad. Remember "read the room?" Well, you're going to need to "read

your life." What's the climate like? How are people reacting to the changes you're making?

Don't be surprised if everyone doesn't understand what you're doing. Try to be thoughtful in how you communicate with others around you about your evolution. You don't want to come across as sanctimonious, smug, or judgmental of others who aren't ready to bounce back. Focus on your own journey and staying the course.

Most importantly, look for rain clouds and potential thunderstorms that may come your way, so that you can try to clear the air.

ALIGNING ANTENNAS.

Not only do you want to know what the weather is, but you want to become attuned to the things you need to look out for, things you may have missed before your setback - things that, in fact, might have led to the setback.

Nanette was a client who came to me when she was going through her divorce. As she worked through the REBOUNDS program, she discovered, as many do in the throes of a relationship that's ending, all the red flags she had missed early in her marriage that signaled her that there was a problem. Aligning her antennas helped Nanette to define very clearly who her ideal mate was, so that when she encountered men who didn't fit into that definition, she could make wise, informed decisions about whether to date them or not.

The same is true for jobs. You can often look back and see where things started to go wrong, if only you'd been paying attention at the time. Align those antennas and start paying close attention to the world around you, so you can see those moments when they happen, in real time, rather than when it's already too late.

ACTIVATING FLIGHT RECORDERS.

One of the best gifts you can give yourself is the gift of a "flight recording," or journaling. Journaling is one way that helps you see things you wouldn't normally see. You can paint a picture that helps you identify patterns in your life, which can help you to head off trouble before it starts.

You can often look back and see where things started to go wrong, if only you'd been paying attention at the time.

It's also a great way to keep yourself honest and stay on track of your progress. When you've said, "I have this goal," it's easy to forget it. But when you've written it down, it's much harder to let it go. And when you write about it regularly, it's impossible to forget, plus you're much more likely to take action to get closer to achieving your goal.

LOCATING AND TURNING ON INTERNAL POWER.

By now you've accepted personal responsibility for your success and bouncing back. Owning your mistakes and taking responsibility for your successes is the single most important, empowered thing you can do to ensure that you achieve your goals, now and in the future. You have the power to change your life - and no one can take that away from you. It's inside you. It's your internal power source. So use it!

LIFTOFF.

It's time. You're ready. You've done the homework. You've dug deep. You've searched your soul. You've done all that you can do (assuming you've done everything I've asked of you). You're ready to soar. No homework, just...soar.

[16]

PUTTING IT ALL TOGETHER

YOU'VE DONE IT! YOU'VE been through all eight steps of REBOUNDS! What do you do now?

STAY THE COURSE

You keep going! Just because you've completed the eight steps, you're not *done*. Remember how I mentioned that it takes six months to a year to "lock in" your new habits? You're going to just keep on working that plan you created. The goal is to stick with it and stay the course.

Sometimes it's easy to continue on with things in the early days, because you're doing more work and it's all very new and interesting. It's harder to stick with it in the long run, because now you're really just implementing the plan.

You'll need to build in metrics and checkpoints to help you stay on track and not stray away from the plans you've so painstakingly created. This is one of the biggest reasons that I put the Trampoline system into place - so that my clients would have access to all the tools and strategies they might need to help them keep their success going, for as long as they needed it.

It's also useful to have someone in your corner, helping you stay accountable.

How Will I Know I'm Done?

I believe that none of us is ever really "done." There will always be things you can improve and work on, there'll always be ways that you can grow as a human being.

> *I believe that none of us is ever really "done." There will always be things you can improve and work on, there'll always be ways that you can grow as a human being.*

But how will you know you're "done" with RE-BOUNDS? When you've fully bounced back and have locked in your new habits to the point where you no longer have to remind yourself to do them, when your new ways of thinking are automatic, rather than things you have to remember, you'll be done.

The great news is that you'll have been through RE-BOUNDS once, so when life hands you another setback...as it always does...you'll have this process to fall back on, again and again, as many times as you need it.

REBOUNDS will work for you in almost any setback in life. So if you used it this time to work on a job situation, if you experience a setback in another area of your life, come back to REBOUNDS and start over.

WHAT TO EXPECT NOW

Now that you've completed REBOUNDS, you can anticipate a recovery from your setback. In fact, you're probably already there (or at least most of the way).

Hopefully you've expelled all or most of the negative emotions that came with your setback and healed the damage that your setback created.

The beauty of REBOUNDS is that it's like a reset button in many ways. It works so well because it helps you avoid going out into the world with the wounds of the past dictating how you live in the present.

Specifically, I'm talking about how, when you've dated someone, for example, and then you break up, you tend to carry the wounds of that relationship into the next one. Make sense? Well, we do that with a lot more than just dating. We do that with jobs, too.

When life hands you another setback...as it always does...you'll have this process to fall back on, again and again, as many times as you need it.

REBOUNDS helps you to release those wounds so that you don't carry them with you to the next thing, which helps you to be much more successful.

How to Expand on Your Success

Now that you're on the other side of this setback, you can look back and see how much progress you've made. Your journals should be excellent resources for this purpose. Take a glimpse back into the pain of that first week, and compare it to a more recent journal.

Be proud of what you've accomplished in these last nine weeks. You've done a lot!

If you want to expand on your success, there's always more that you can do. If you've done the DIY version of RE-BOUNDS, then working with a coach can be a wonderful next step to continuing your journey of growth and self-actualization. You'll realize that you've really only just begun scratch the surface of all that you are capable of accomplishing.

More Resources

There's always more to do, and if you truly want to become a master of the bounceback, you'll want to consider some of the following options.

Online Community

Our online community of "bouncers" can be found on Facebook. Whether you join the regular group or become a client and gain access to the private client group and Trampoline system, you'll find a wonderful community of supportive, helpful people who are going through the exact same steps you are, working on their own setbacks and bouncebacks. You'll be in good company.

The REBOUNDS Course

I've set up a companion course to help you work through the REBOUNDS program, if you're struggling with doing the program from a book or want more. The course includes actual training components (backed by solid andragogy and instructional design), as well as worksheets, some of the metrics you'll need already set up, and a journal.

The course is designed to be self-paced, but you won't be going through it alone.

In the fully DIY track, you'll have access to talk with fellow bouncers who are working through the same step you are.

In the DIY + Virtual Coaching track, my coaches and I will be checking in on you periodically through the Trampoline system, providing helpful guidance, insight, and encouragement along the way, as well as holding office hours so that you can come to the table with your questions and get live answers. At the beginning of this book, I told you that you wouldn't be alone in this process, and I meant that. My team and I are just an email away. Plus, when you take the course, you'll also have access to our private client community, so you'll have their support as well.

Individual Coaching

If you want the best of all worlds, then you can apply to be a private, one-on-one coaching client of mine, and I'll take you through the REBOUNDS program personally. We'll work together on the phone, talking through your setback, your challenges, and any place that you get stuck. You'll still have access to the Trampoline system tools, and you'll get a customized version of the program, with metrics and homework designed specifically for you. And you'll also have access to the online community.

If you'd like to apply to be a private, one-on-one coaching client, visit: http://bouncebackartist.com/coaching-application and complete the application there. We'll have a conversation to ensure it's a good fit, and if it is, then we'll get started right away.

The most important thing is that you shouldn't stop here. There's always more growing to be done, more joy to be found, and more tweaks you can do to make your life better. Be a constant work in progress and you'll be amazed at what you can accomplish.

I believe in you.

Appendix A
The ACE Score

1. Did a parent or other adult in the household often or very often swear at you, insult you, put you down, or humiliate you? Act in a way that made you afraid that you might be physically hurt?
   No___ If Yes, enter 1 ___

2. Did a parent or other adult in the household often or very often push, grab, slap, or throw something at you? Ever hit you so hard that you had marks or were injured?
   No___ If Yes, enter 1 ___

3. Did an adult or person at least 5 years older than you ever touch or fondle you or have you touch their body in a sexual way? Attempt or actually have oral, anal, or vaginal intercourse with you?
   No___ If Yes, enter 1 ___

4. Did you often or very often feel that no one in your family loved you or thought you were important or special? Or your family didn't look out for each other, feel close to each other, or support each other?
   No___ If Yes, enter 1 ___

5. Did you often or very often feel that you didn't have enough to eat, had to wear dirty clothes, and had no

one to protect you? Or your parents were too drunk
or high to take care of you or take you to the doctor if
you needed it?

No___ If Yes, enter 1 __

6. Were your parents ever separated or divorced?

No___ If Yes, enter 1 __

7. Was your mother or stepmother: Often or very often
pushed, grabbed, slapped, or had something thrown at
her? Or sometimes, often, or very often kicked, bitten,
hit with a fist, or hit with something hard? Or ever repeatedly hit over at least a few minutes or threatened
with a gun or knife?

No___ If Yes, enter 1 __

8. Did you live with anyone who was a problem drinker
or alcoholic, or who used street drugs?

No___ If Yes, enter 1 __

9. Was a household member depressed or mentally ill, or
did a household member attempt suicide?

No___ If Yes, enter 1 __

10. Did a household member go to prison?

No___ If Yes, enter 1 __

Now add up your "Yes" answers: ____
This is your ACE Score.

Appendix B
The Resilience Score[18]

Please circle the most accurate answer <u>under each statement:</u>

1. **I believe that my mother loved me when I was little.**
   Definitely True
   Probably True
   Not Sure
   Probably Not True
   Definitely Not True

2. **I believe that my father loved me when I was little.**
   Definitely True
   Probably True
   Not Sure
   Probably Not True
   Definitely Not True

3. **When I was little, other people helped my mother and father take care of me and they seemed to love me.**
   Definitely True
   Probably True
   Not Sure
   Probably Not True
   Definitely Not True

4. **I've heard that when I was an infant someone in my family enjoyed playing with me, and I enjoyed it, too.**
Definitely True
Probably True
Not Sure
Probably Not True
Definitely Not True

5. **When I was a child, there were relatives in my family who made me feel better if I was sad or worried.**
Definitely True
Probably True
Not Sure
Probably Not True
Definitely Not True

6. **When I was a child, neighbors or my friends' parents seemed to like me.**
Definitely True
Probably True
Not Sure
Probably Not True
Definitely Not True

7. **When I was a child, teachers, coaches, youth leaders or ministers were there to help me.**
Definitely True
Probably True
Not Sure
Probably Not True
Definitely Not True

8. **Someone in my family cared about how I was do-**

ing in school.
Definitely True
Probably True
Not Sure
Probably Not True
Definitely Not True

9. **My family, neighbors and friends talked often about making our lives better.**
Definitely True
Probably True
Not Sure
Probably Not True
Definitely Not True

10. **We had rules in our house and were expected to keep them.**
Definitely True
Probably True
Not Sure
Probably Not True
Definitely Not True

11. **When I felt really bad, I could almost always find someone I trusted to talk to.**
Definitely True
Probably True
Not Sure
Probably Not True
Definitely Not True

12. **As a youth, people noticed that I was capable and could get things done.**
Definitely True
Probably True
Not Sure

Probably Not True
Definitely Not True

13. I was independent and a go-getter.
Definitely True
Probably True
Not Sure
Probably Not True
Definitely Not True

14. I believed that life is what you make it.
Definitely True
Probably True
Not Sure
Probably Not True
Definitely Not True

How many of these 14 protective factors did I have as a child and youth? (How many of the 14 were circled "Definitely True" or "Probably True"?) _____

Of these circled, how many are still true for me? _____

This is your Resilience Score.

ACKNOWLEDGEMENTS

THIS BOOK HAS BEEN in the making for longer than my first book was, but the list of those I must thank for aiding me in the process of completing this work is considerably shorter, mostly because unlike my first book, which was somewhat of a noisy process, I wrote this book much more quietly and reflectively, and without much input until the end.

> *"Alone we can do so little,*
> *together we can do so much."*
>
> - Helen Keller

My husband, Leonardo, provides me with a seemingly endless supply of support, encouragement, and belief in my ability to do great things. He's been there when I was going through my setbacks, and let me support him when he experienced his own. He is up for every adventure, is the consummate husband, partner, and best friend, and is the only person I could ever imagine spending my life with. I'm awfully grateful that he seems to feel the same way. Leo, you are magic. You are my light. You make me a better human.

While they can't read, I must also thank Gus, my Chief Barketing Officer, and Max, my Vice President of Bouncing, who were by my side for the writing of this book. Whenever

I needed a break, their fuzzy faces and pure hearts gave me a much-needed reset.

"None of us is as smart as all of us."
- Ken Blanchard

Without Lynn Swayze, I may never have written this book, or at least it would have taken much longer to finish. She created the scaffolding that allowed me to let knowledge flow into book form quickly, and helped shape the concept of the business that is growing out of it.

I'm grateful to Jeremy Pope, who, upon hearing me describe my work, said, "I'm thinking...the BounceBack Artist is a great brand for what you do." I was typically, stubbornly resistant, but bought the domain name anyway. I'm glad that I did.

I would be remiss if I didn't thank my friends, colleagues, and clients who read the early drafts of this book and provided incredibly valuable, helpful feedback and suggestions, particularly Shelli Herman, Ben Cope, Stephanie Hinderer, and Brande Plotnick, as well as the extraordinary individuals who took the time to write about their support of the book on the cover and inside pages.

An extra special thank you to Ruth Hatch, who gave me invaluable feedback, an eagle eye, and a gentle reminder that conjunctions really ought not begin sentences.

A deeply special and heartfelt thank you goes to my friend and mentor, Robert Thomas Bethel, who gave the effusive encouragement my ego desired, and mysteriously managed to send it exactly when a roadblock or challenge reared its head. Bob, you are a fount of wisdom, exceptional business advice, and endlessly entertaining stories. I am endlessly grateful to you for your generosity and your belief in me.

I'm also appreciative of the many setbacks in my own life that taught me so much and launched a system I genuinely believe will help countless others.

I'm eternally grateful for my clients who shared their setback and rebound journeys with me and trusted me to help guide them back. They say it's important to love your work. I definitely love mine, and I love it in part because I have such extraordinary clients. Thank you for continuously helping shape me into a better coach.

Finally, thank you, dear reader. If you weren't interested in these words, I would have no reason to write. Thank you for giving me the time it took you to read this book. I hope that I lived up to the expectation and the hope that this book promised you. May you bounce back from all your setbacks with grace and fortitude.

- Susan

ABOUT THE AUTHOR

SUSAN BARONCINI-MOE IS AN executive coach and business leader with over eighteen years' experience. With a Master's degree in Social Psychology, a MicroMasters in Instructional Design and Technology, training from NLP Comprehensive, Nightingale-Conant's "Lead the Field" Executive Success Coaching, and Wellcoaches, Susan is one of the most dynamic, well-rounded, results-driven coaches in the marketplace today.

The author of the bestselling book, *Business in Blue Jeans: How to Have a Successful Business on Your Own Terms, in Your Own Style*, Susan has worked with clients on four continents in a wide range of industries. She is a sought-after strategist, and she and her businesses have been featured on ABC and in Redbook magazine, USA Today, MSN Living, Yahoo Finance, Investors Business Daily, Social Media Examiner, American Express Open Forum, Chicago Tribune, Indianapolis Star, and more.

Susan's business blog, Business in Blue Jeans, has been listed by several notable resources as one of the best blogs for entrepreneurs and business owners. She has been the host of four popular YouTube shows and podcasts.

Susan held the Guinness World Records® title for the world's longest uninterrupted live webcast for two and a half years. She has served on the Board of Directors for the Junior League of Indianapolis, has tried over 100 hobbies, plays the violin, and travels the globe with her Uruguayan rock star husband, Leo.

Susan has read over 2900 books on the subjects of personal development and personal growth, business, leadership, entrepreneurship, psychology, coaching, wellness, health, wellbeing, networking, marketing, strategic planning, relationships, interpersonal dynamics, philosophy, and management.

References

1. Felitti, V. J., Et al. (1998). Relationship of Childhood Abuse and Household Dysfunction to Many of the Leading Causes of Death in Adults. American Journal of Preventative Medicine, 14(4), 245-258.

2. Disease Control and Prevention, C. F. (2016, April 1). Adverse Childhood Experiences (ACEs). Retrieved September 1, 2018, from https://www.samhsa.gov/capt/practicing-effective-prevention/ prevention-behavioral-health/adverse-childhood-experiences

3. Staff, I. (2018, July 09). Top 6 Reasons New Businesses Fail. Retrieved September 1, 2018, from https://www.investopedia.com/ slide-show/top-6-reasons-new-businesses-fail/

4. NCAA (2018, April 23). Estimated probability of competing in professional athletics. Retrieved September 1, 2018, from http://www.ncaa.org/about/resources/research/ estimated-probability-competing-professional-athletics

5. American Psychological Association. (n.d.). Divorce. Retrieved September 1, 2018, from https://www.apa.org/topics/divorce/

6. Hellebuyck, M., Et al. (2017). Mind the Workplace. Mental Health America. Retrieved September 1, 2018, from http://www.mental-healthamerica.net/sites/default/files/Mind the Workplace - MHA Workplace Health Survey 2017 FINAL.PDF

7. Peoplewave. (2017, November 20). 1 in 4 Employees Cries After Workplace Performance Reviews and 10 More Facts About Em-

ployee... Retrieved September 1, 2018, from https://medium.com/@Peoplewave/one-in-four-employees-cry-after-workplace-performance-reviews-and-10-more-facts-about-employee-c7ff-7037c4f5

8. Half, Robert (2019, January 03). Australian Salary Guide & Survey. Retrieved September 9, 2018, from https://www.roberthalf.com.au/research-insights/salary- guide

9. Morris, A. (2017, October 16). Heading for the exit: The impact of negative performance reviews. Retrieved January 16, 2019, from https://www.roberthalf.com.au/blog/employers/heading-exit-impact-negative- performance -reviews

10. Atkinson, R. P., & Harrington, T. L. (1986). Final Technical Report NCC 2-272 Contributions to Workload of Rotational Optical Transformations (Rep.). Reno, NV: NASA/Fast Motion Perception Laboratory, Department of Psychology, University of Nevada. https://ntrs.nasa.gov/archive/nasa/casi.ntrs.nasa.gov/19860011635.pdf

11. Lally, P., Jaarsveld, C. H., Potts, H. W., & Wardle, J. (2009). How are habits formed: Modelling habit formation in the real world. European Journal of Social Psychology, 40(6), 998-1009. doi:10.1002/ejsp.674

12. Chodron, P. (2006). Practicing Peace in Times of War: A Buddhist Perspective. Shambhala.

13. Baroncini-Moe, S., & Watkins, L. (2018, January 26). Stress Relief and Meditation - An Interview with Light Watkins. Retrieved January 26, 2018, from https://youtu.be/mm9h5lEF81M

14. Hendrix, H. (2008). Getting the love you want: A guide for couples. New York: St. Martins Griffin.

15. Dyer, W. (2017, November 16). Love Your Enemy? Retrieved from https://www.drwaynedyer.com/blog/love-your-enemy/

16. Doran, G. T. (1981). "There's a S.M.A.R.T. Way to Write Management's Goals and Objectives", Management Review, Vol. 70, Issue 11, pp. 35-36.

17. Dunbar, B. (n.d.). Countdown 101. Retrieved from https://www.nasa.gov/mission_pages/shuttle/launch/countdown101.html

18. Rains, M., McClinn, K., & Southern Kennebec Healthy Start (2006). What's Your Resilience Score? Retrieved September 1, 2018, from https://www.acrf.org/assets/courses-pdf/course/ACES3ResScoreHO.pdf